EXPLORING PREHISTORIC ENGLAND

Alfred the Great
Jeffreys
A History of Europe 1450–1660
Modern British History 1815–1964
England Under the Yorkists and Tudors 1471–1603

Dead Men's Fingers
Death Has a Thousand Entrances
The Man With No Bones

EXPLORING
PREHISTORIC
ENGLAND

P. J. Helm

ROBERT HALE . LONDON

ISBN 0 7091 2104 0

Robert Hale & Company
63 Old Brompton Road
London S.W.7

PRINTED IN GREAT BRITAIN BY
REDWOOD PRESS LIMITED
TROWBRIDGE, WILTSHIRE

The treasures of time lie high, in Urnes, Coynes, and Monuments, scarce below the roots of some vegetables—

Sir Thomas Browne (1605–1682). *Hydriotaphia, Urne Buriall; or, a Discourse of the Sepulchrall Urnes lately found in Norfolk.*

To
John

CONTENTS

ILLUSTRATIONS

MAPS AND PLANS

PICTURE CREDITS

Ministry of Public Building and Works: 1, 2, 3, 4, 5, 6, 9, 11, 18, 19; Aerofilms Limited: 7, 8, 13, 14, 15, 16, 17; Bodleian Library: 10; Central Office of Information: 12.

INTRODUCTION

This book is an attempt to provide the ordinary traveller with a simplified outline of English prehistory as at present understood and to link this with a description of some of the more important sites, a selection of others worth seeing, and information as to how to reach these places. (Ordnance Survey 1-inch map references are given in brackets after the names of principal sites.)

Is there any justification for such a book? I think there is. People today are more aware than ever before of the history beneath their feet. The B.B.C. finds it worthwhile to mount an expensive investigation of the largest artificial mound in Europe. A Sunday newspaper devotes a colour supplement to work at the reputed site of Arthur's Camelot. Cheap transport brings an increasing number of people each year to the better-known sites.

Yet the interest indicated by these facts is largely an uncomprehending one. A clear picture of what happened in England before the Roman Conquest is not part of the easily-accessible store of general knowledge. The interested traveller gets by as best he can on a sparse supply of old-fashioned ideas, typified by such phrases as 'cave men', 'ancient Britons' and 'Druids'.

Accurate information remains locked away behind the scientific terminology of the professional archaeologist. Occasionally an expert produces a brilliant, simple outline, but this is unfortunately a rare occurrence. Archaeologists are fierce and will tear to pieces one of their number who makes an insecure generalisation.

An outsider can afford to take more risks. One of the aims of this book is to bridge the gap, to push back the frontiers of general knowledge, to suggest that social history can begin, not with the Roman Conquest, but at the very least with the New Stone Age, 3,500 years earlier. To this end simplification has been attempted to an extent that will, rightly, pain the expert, but may help the traveller.

THE OLD AND MIDDLE STONE AGES:
from the Earliest Men to about 3500 B.C.

... everything which has come down to us from heathendom is wrapped in a thick fog; it belongs to a space of time which we cannot measure.

Professor Rasmus Nyerup (1759–1829)

THE OLD STONE AGE

The Old Stone Age *(Palaeolithic)* men, hunters and food-gatherers, may have lived in Britain—not yet an island—500,000 years ago.

This is a date so distant as to be quite different from those with which we are accustomed to deal. It is not like last Thursday. It would be cosy if we could still accept the views of Dr. John Lightfoot, who, in the seventeenth century, believed that he had proved that "man was created by the Trinity on October 23, 4004 B.C., at nine o'clock in the morning". Lacking Dr. Lightfoot's certainty, we must try to take the modern chronology by surprise as it were, if we are to catch its significance.

To put it in one way: the Trojan War, that distant struggle of gods and heroes—and real men—which stands at the threshold of European history, took place about 3,000 years ago. Suppose it had happened about twelve hours ago, about breakfast time? Then the dawn of the Old Stone Age would still have been three years ago: Hitler, on the other hand, would only have been dead ten minutes.

If the length of time is immense, the rate of change was as inconceivably slow. For all but the last 30,000 years the nonprofessional may regard our past history as an almost unchanging picture, faintly diversified at long intervals by the languid pulsations of the ice sheet that covered the greater part of the country, by certain minute refinements in the flint instruments available, and by the arrival of hunters of varying stocks, some of which perhaps—but one cannot be sure—may have been in the direct line of true men.

These, true men or sub-men, roamed Britain south of the ice-south, that is to say south of a line from the Severn estuary to the estuary of the Thames. The total population was not more than

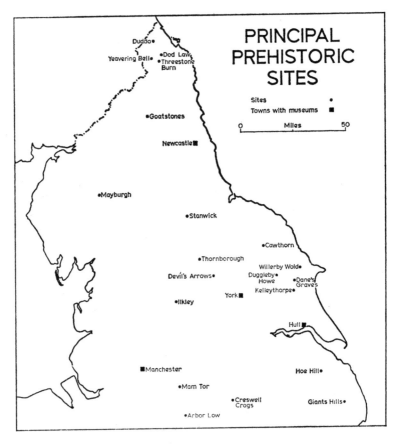

The North of England

200 or 300. Like the Eskimoes of the far north today, these people were compelled to hunt over very large areas if they were to gather sufficient food for a family group of perhaps thirty persons. Less than a dozen such groups made up the people of Britain—a Britain which indeed did not yet exist, for what is now the North Sea and the English Channel was then dry land. Southern Britain was only a north-western extension of Europe. The people lived brief lives. Evidence from other parts of the continent suggests that not more than one in five reached the age of 30.

A great many flints, two bones from a skull and part of a wooden spear are virtually all that remain from those cold, hard times. One must make the most of them.

The spear, a 12-inch yew-wood point hardened by fire, was preserved in a peaty loam at Clacton. As one looks at this small piece of vegetable matter (now in the Department of Geology, British Museum) it becomes clear that flint appears to us to have been the characteristic material of prehistoric man *because it has survived*. Skins and furs, wooden windbreaks and implements, these almost certainly played a most important part, perhaps even *the* most important, in 'Stone Age' life. Here, right at the start, one is brought up against the most fundamental limitation of prehistory. What the archaeologist can deduce has been decided for him by what has survived.

Flint implements can be made in one of two main ways. The simpler and more obvious is to take a piece and strike at it until the original lump has been reduced to the desired size and shape. It is the way in which a sculptor carves a statue, peeling off, as it were, the stone casing in order to reveal the figure concealed within. So, too, primitive man chipped his flint to expose the coretool hidden inside the rough block.

The earliest type of core-tool was a pear-shaped affair about 6 inches long and 2 inches in diameter at its widest part, the base. In a museum it is likely to be labelled as a 'hand-axe', which is, for the amateur, misleading. The hand-axe was really a general purpose tool. The round butt fitted the palm of the hand, the fingers gripped the sloping sides and the heavy, pointed flint could then be used for cutting, piercing, grubbing and hacking. These men held a whole chest of tools in their rough but clearly not unskilful hands.

The earliest core-tools are known as Abevillian, from Abbeville near Amiens in northern France. A later, more refined, hand-axe is labelled Acheulian, from St. Acheul, also near Amiens.

The fragments of skull already mentioned are seen as coming from this second, Acheulian, period. These, the earliest known human remains in Britain, were found at Swanscombe in Kent. There, in 1935–6, a dentist, A. T. Marston, discovered two bones of a skull, associated with remains of elephant, rhinoceros and red deer, and with flint hand-axes of the Acheulian type. The skull was that of someone 20 to 25 years of age. The contours and thickness of the bones suggest a head not so very different from that of modern man. The face and jaws may have been rather heavier. Swanscombe man, living 250,000 years ago was in the direct line—or not far from it—that leads to *Homo sapiens*. He is the first Briton that we know and the greater part of prehistory is over before we have a companion to set beside him. For this reason the rather undramatic remains, now in the Department of Geology, British Museum, are worth inspection.

A more sophisticated method of flint-working is to detach flakes from the raw lump and then work on these fragments. A distinctive type of these flake tools was first found in East Anglia and is known as Clactonian. In age they represented a parallel development to the Acheulian. The wooden implement already described was probably shaped by one of these flint flakes used as a spoke-shave.

This world, represented only by a handful of bones and flints, glimpsed for a moment, was destroyed by the relentless advance of the ice, perhaps 100,000 years ago. When the fourth Ice Age—the last so far—began to draw to a close and the ice retreated once more, southern Britain was occupied by the first 'real' men. Between 35,000 and 20,000 years ago they established themselves in the bare landscape which was for them the fringe of the habitable world.

Once again small groups of hunters worked their way back and forth across the British tundra. In the summer they lived in the open, in the winter they lived in the mouths of caves—where these existed. The point is worth making, for the cave-man is such a strongly established figure in cartoon- and joke-land. In Britain, life in caves must always have been the exception rather than the rule. And where caves did exist they were occupied, on and off, for thousands of years. In terms of sheer numbers the cave-population was at its greatest in the comparatively civilized period of the Roman occupation.

The caves have survived, while the more general but less durable shelters have not. Once again, we are at the mercy of chance, of the material evidence that has not perished.

There are three main groups of caves. On the Gower peninsula the most famous is that at Paviland (SS/437859). Here the first Old Stone Age burial was discovered by Dean Buckland. He thought the bones were those of a woman and called her 'the Red Lady of Paviland'. In fact 'the Red Lady' was a man in his twenties. More significantly, the Dean decided that 'she' was a Romano-British woman. He could not accept the fact that a human being might possibly have lived at the date implied by the bones of the extinct animals—mammoth, hairy rhinoceros, cave bear and so on—amongst which it lay. Here is another limitation on the interpretation of prehistoric evidence. The Dean was blinkered by his theology; modern archaeologists may be equally confined within their social or political philosophies.

The Goat's Hole where 'the Red Lady' was buried was once a desirable residence with a natural chimney and a south-facing terrace, beyond which there was a coastal plain. Today the sea has risen and there is no plain. Do not attempt to visit the cave, it is easy to be cut off at high tide.

The cave, when discovered, was full of an accumulated litter of animal bones, flint scrapers and—a new material—bone pins and awls. The most interesting object was an egg-shaped pendant, carved from a deformity in a mammoth's tusk. The most interesting, that is to say, apart from the 'Red Lady' himself. He was 'Red' because his skeleton has been covered with powdered red ochre. This approximated to the colour of blood and the deduction is that it was symbolic of life. The head was missing, and at the upper and lower end of the skeleton a stone had been placed. There are no magical cave paintings in Britain such as delight the visitor to France or Spain, but at Gower there is a clear indication that already religious magic, or magical religion, was well-established.

The second group of caves is at Creswell Crags (SK/535742) in the Peak District of Derbyshire. The valley itself is attractive and worth a detour, though the finds are in the British Museum and the Manchester Museum. Take road A60 (Worksop-Mansfield) and turn west 4 miles from Worksop along B6042 to the village of Creswell. The valley is just east of the village and the road runs through it.

These caves were occupied for about 100,000 years, from the days before the arrival of *Homo sapiens* down to at least Roman

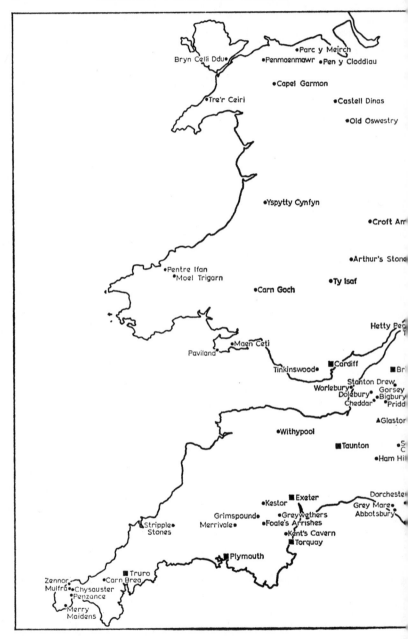

The S

PRINCIPAL PREHISTORIC SITES

Sites   ●
Towns with museum   ■

●West Rudham

■Norwich

●Burrough Hill

●Grime's Graves
■Thetford

■Cambridge
●Wandlebury

Bredon

●King's Men

●Belas Knap

●Therfield Heath

Colchester■

■Oxford

●Wheathampstead

●●Uffington
Wayland's Smithy

ury

dmill
Hill●●Avebury
oury●●West Kennet

■Devizes
tleton

●Combe
Gibbet

●Silchester

■London

●Ladle Hill

●Kit's Coty House
●Oldbury

●Julieberrie's
Grave

anton●

●Stonehenge
●Danebury

●●Anstiebury
Abinger

●Winterbourne
Stoke

isbury■

●Martin Down

●Bokerley

●Butser Hill

●Knowlton

Badbury

●Cissbury

istbury●

```
0          Miles          50
|————————————————————|
```

times. The main caves are Church Hole on the south side of the valley, Mother Grundy's Parlour at the east end, and Pin Hole Cave and Robin Hood's Cave, both on the north side.

From Pin Hole came a piece of bone engraved with a phallic human figure, bow in hand and wearing an animal's mask. In Robin Hood's Cave there was found a bone engraved with the head of a horse, the best example of British Old Stone Age art— and it must be admitted that there is hardly any competition for that title.

The third area of cave life lies in the south-west. In Devon remains have been found in caves at Brixham (Windmill Hill Cave) and at Torquay (Kent's Cavern). A selection of the finds can be seen in the museum at Torquay.

More important, and certainly more atmospheric, are the Mendip Caves in Somerset. At the west end there is a group of caves of which one, Gough's Cave (ST/466538), has a small museum attached to it, containing finds made in the area. To reach it, turn east off road A38 (Bristol-Bridgwater) along A371 (Axbridge and Wells). At Cheddar take the road towards Cheddar Gorge. At the other end of the Mendips there is Wookey Hole and the Hyaena Den (ST/531480). Wookey itself was not occupied until the Iron Age, but is the most dramatic of the caves. The Hyaena Den lies 60 yards to the south. Both caves can be reached by turning north off the A371 as soon as one leaves Wells. In the Hyaena Den a prodigious number of animal bones were found, the remains of mammoths, woolly rhinoceros, bison, giant elk, reindeer, cave bear and, from a later date, wild horses. A selection of these finds is in the Bristol Museum.

The inhabitants of southern Britain who have left their traces in these caves were not the shambling, back-bowed figures of the strip cartoon. The image built up from remains here and on the Continent is of men tall, long-limbed, the shoulders broad, the hips rather narrow, the hands and feet large in proportion—in general perhaps like the Red Indian (though, of course, there is no evidence as to the colour of the skin). Their skulls indicate a high head, long and narrow, with strong wide cheekbones. It has been observed that this type is still common in the remote moorland areas of Denbigh and Plynlymmon. It is not impossible that biological traces of our earliest ancestors survive in these areas, where brown eyes and dark hair predominate.[1]

[1] See H. J. Fleure, *The Natural History of Man in Britain* (Collins 1959), Plate VIII, Mr. J. James.

The last men of the Old Stone Age, living perhaps 15,000 years ago, had at their disposal a variety of implements developed over the millenia, which, when compared with the primitive hand-axe, represent a great advance in technology.

Flint was worked into knives, gravers, scrapers and prickers. A surprising amount is known about the manufacture of these instruments. The information is derived partly from the evidence of flakes and pressure-marks, partly from the observation of practices that have survived into historical times in Mexico, among the Australian aborigines and at home in Norfolk, where flint-knappers were still at work in the fifties.

The crudest method of working is to dash the flint against a larger stone. More delicately, one may hold the stone in the hand, pressed against the knee or the ground, and strike it. More sophisticated still is the technique known as 'pressure-flaking'. Elegant flakes can be produced by using, not stone against stone, but bone or wood against flint and by carefully varying the angle at which the pressure is applied. The Suffolk flint-knappers used a combination of techniques, starting with a huge hammer-stone weighing about 3 pounds and then changing to a stone of only a couple of ounces when trimming the flakes.

Once the techniques have been mastered, production is more rapid than might be supposed. In seventeenth-century Mexico it was recorded that a worker could produce 100 obsidian knife blades in an hour. In Australia an aborgine could make a spear-head from bottle glass in ten minutes. In the days—still within living memory—when East Anglia made gun-flints for export to West Africa, the output ran at the rate of 15,000 a month. As against these figures, one must remember that many British pre-historic flint-working areas are littered with spoilt stones and that it is on record that in North Queensland a native might strike 300 flakes before he made exactly the blade that he desired.

Other materials available included bone and ivory, which could be carved into fish-hooks, spear and arrow heads, bracelets, spear-throwers, and a peculiar decorated rod with a hole at one end, which may have been a prosaic arrow-straightener or may have served a more dramatic purpose as a symbol of authority (*bâton de commandement*).

The Old Stone Age people were thus now able to work flint and bone, to prepare flesh for food and skins for clothing, to manufacture weapons for hunting, and probably to knot fishing-lines and nets. They had developed the first stages of art, of religion, of technology, and by the use of shelters and fires they had begun, if ever so slightly, to create an artificial environment for themselves.

This apparently stable culture came to a comparatively abrupt end about 12,000 years ago. The climate changed, the universe of Old Stone Age man was destroyed. The retreating ice sheets disappeared and Britain entered a time when the climate was warmer and drier than at the present day, known as the Boreal phase. The thin tundra vegetation was replaced by forests of birch and pine, the place of the reindeer was taken by the red deer and the wild ox, the aurochs.

About 6000 B.C. the climate, though remaining warm, grew much wetter, the Atlantic phase. Birch and pine were replaced, at least in the south, by damp forests of oak and elm, lime, alder and hazel. The sea level rose and the North Sea area, which in Boreal times had been covered with pine-woods and marshes, became indeed the North Sea, while the English Channel at last severed Britain from the continent.

THE MIDDLE STONE AGE 8000 to 3500 B.C.

In spite of his fires and shelters, man was still very much at the mercy of his environment when the Old Stone Age existence gave place to the Middle Stone Age (the Mesolithic period). The greatly changed climate meant a greatly changed culture.

The people themselves may not have been very different from their predecessors—no physical remains have been found—and may indeed have been in some cases their descendants, but they were forced by circumstances to adopt different methods of hunting and food-gathering. It looks as though these methods originated in continental Europe and then spread by land (before the wetter Atlantic period) to Britain. Eastern England must be pictured not as an area in its own right, but rather as the western rim of these new European 'forest cultures', and the new men must be seen as coming by land, perhaps picking their way through fresh-water marshes. (Twenty-five miles off the Norfolk coast part of a Mesolithic fish-spear was found buried in peat formed in one of these marshes.)

Three inter-related cultures appear to have 'invaded' Britain. From Scandinavia came the men called the Maglemose people, after a site at Mullerup in Denmark (*magle mose* means big bog). From north-east France the Tardenoisians (so called from La Fèreen-Tardenois in the department of Aisne) moved into south-east England. Very much later a third group settled in Scotland around the Forth estuary and along the west coast from Oban to Kirkcudbright. These Scottish settlements date from between 4000 and 3000 B.C.

The Middle Stone Age peoples form a most important link in the prehistory of Britain, but they make little impact on the ordinary traveller, for the remains which they have left are extraordinarily unimpressive. There is usually nothing to see at a Mesolithic site and, visiting a museum, one is most likely to be faced with rows of very small flints (microliths) which do not make much of a show in a glass case. The natural reaction is to hurry on to something more dramatic.

To do so would be a pity. These apparent parings, looking like giant nail-clippings, were manufactured by pressure-flaking. Very skilful pressure was applied with a piece of bone or wood until the flake, itself perhaps only half an inch in length, broke off the larger piece of flint and in doing so acquired an accurately determined shape.

The flakes could then be carefully fitted into wood or bone handles to make a wide range of instruments or weapons. These objects of a composite structure, created by fitting together a number of parts, represent a great advance in technique. It is the first short step to modern machinery and the production line.

Man's energies were still devoted almost entirely to the primary task of finding enough food to keep himself alive. The climatic changes had made life a little less harsh and had opened up many areas hitherto covered by ice, with the result that Britain now supported a larger population. There were more Mesolithic men than there had ever been Old Stone Age men, but the total was still very small. It has been estimated that the numbers rose from those of a small village to those of a small town—perhaps 10,000 to 20,000 in the whole of Britain. Man was still a hunter and collector of his food, requiring large areas from which to support the family group.

New instruments helped to maintain this larger population. Mesolithic man had at his disposal fish-spears and harpoons, sledges, canoes and paddles, and a new hunting weapon, the bow and arrow. In forest areas the stone chopper was provided with a wooden haft, thus attaining approximately the shape of a modern axe.

The Mesolithic people hunted—in order of importance—the red deer, the wild ox, the roe deer and the wild pig, together with a host of smaller game, foxes and martens, wolves and wild cats, birds and beavers. They also grubbed for edible roots, using for this purpose a sort of mattock made from an antler and fitted with a wooden handle. And above all, wherever possible, they fished.

How they fished! In parts of Denmark they seem to have lived exclusively on shell-fish, tossing the shells out of the back-door (figuratively speaking) until their homes were buried in great piles of shells—an untidy habit which has led to their acquiring the unattractive name of 'the kitchen-midden people'. In England shell-fish do not figure so largely and ordinary fish bones do not, perhaps fortunately, last long, but it is significant how often Mesolithic sites were close to sheets of fresh water or to the sea shore.

This is something of a composite picture. The life on individual sites varied greatly, depending on the local environment. A little is known of three different types of site in Britain—which, incidentally, provide the oldest surviving traces of artificial dwellings to be found in Britain.

In Sussex at Selmeston and in Surrey at Farnham and Abinger, camp sites have been found which date from this period. The site at Abinger (TQ/112459) lies 1¼ miles south-east of the junction of road A25 (Guildford-Dorking) and B2126, in a field to the west of Abinger Manor Farm. The remains of a pit-dwelling can be seen and there is a museum on the site—always a more satisfactory arrangement than when site and finds are separated by hundreds of miles. Since Mesolithic sites are usually so unrewarding for the traveller this one is well worth a visit.

A pit 14 feet by 10 feet had been scraped out of the soft Greensand to a depth of 3 feet. At the deeper western end there was a pile of stones and signs of a fire. Here was, presumably, the hearth. On the eastern side there was a ledge which probably indicates a sleeping area. (This three-fold division into areas for cooking, sleeping and general activities recurs frequently in later prehistoric settlements until at last it becomes a permanent feature of the historic peasant's hut.) There were two post-holes at the western end which would have held supports for some simple sloping roof of brushwood. Close by the pit there was a spring. Something like 8,000 microliths were found in and around the site, which was occupied about 5000 B.C.

Other Mesolithic sites in southern England are similar to the one at Abinger—irregular hollows scraped out of soft ground to a depth of about 3 feet, their size ranging from 14 feet by 10 feet to 30 by 15 feet. One must imagine the complete affair as no more than a rough shelter of sticks and branches, half below ground and half above, with an opening to the south protected by a curtain of skins. The area around these irregular scrapings is always thick with microliths: at a site near Selborne 3,000 implements and 82,000 flakes were found within an area only 30 feet by 20.

Besides the places already referred to, Mesolithic sites are known in the south at Downtown in Wiltshire and in Dorset. In the latter county forty sites have been discovered, the majority around what is now Poole harbour.

In other areas the Mesolithic people clearly took over the caves already brought into use by the Old Stone Age hunters, since it is not uncommon for a layer of Mesolithic remains to overlay the older deposits of their predecessors. This is true of some of the caves already described, while another example is King Arthur's Cave (SO/545155) in Herefordshire. Turn right $2\frac{1}{2}$ miles north of Monmouth off road A40 (Monmouth-Ross). One mile down this minor road turn right again. The cave is on the left beyond a quarry. It was occupied from about 25,000 B.C. to about A.D. 240. Finds from the cave can be seen in the museums at Cheltenham and Gloucester.

A rather different site—and one that has provided a great deal of information—was discovered at Star Carr (TA/027809) in the North Riding of Yorkshire, 4 or 5 miles south of Scarborough and one mile north-east of the crossroads A64 and A1039. There is, though, nothing to be seen at the site: the material found is now divided between the Natural History Museum in London, the Cambridge Museum of Archaeology and the local Scarborough Museum.

When the Ice Age came to an end the melt water formed a lake in the vale of Pickering to the south of Star Carr, a lake which gradually shrank into a chain of freshwater bogs and meres. A party of early Mesolithic hunters built a camp on the north shore of one of these meres and occupied it for a number of seasons.

A platform of birchwood was built up at the water's edge and huts—or perhaps tents—were set up on it. Two birch-tree trunks jutted out at right angles to form a little jetty and a wooden paddle has been found, though there is no sign of the boat which it propelled. The area of the settlement was about 240 square yards, and it is likely that several families camped there during the winter season, moving off each summer. Perhaps that was when the boat, or boats, disappeared.

Most of the evidence for the description given above of Mesolithic man's life has come from the rich finds at Star Carr. Peculiar to the site were two unusual and exciting finds. One was a collection of rolls of birch bark. This bark produces a sticky substance rather like pitch and there is no doubt that the settlers used this early form of glue to hold microliths in their wooden seating, for flints with birch glue still on them have been recovered.

The glue is a practical, technical discovery. The other surprising find lies in a different area of intellectual activity. Twenty stag frontlets—the upper part of the skull together with the antlers—were discovered, which had been lightened and perforated so that they might be worn on the forehead. They were used either in ritual hunting ceremonies or as a form of camouflage when actually on the trail.

It stirs the imagination to recall that at Abbot's Bromley, Staffordshire, the 'deermen' still dance every year, holding the frontlets of deer on sticks before their bodies. About 300 generations separate the Abbot's Bromley dancers from the Star Carr men: the human links between the two could be easily seated in a small village hall.

While technically so much in advance of their Old Stone Age counterparts, the Mesolithic hunter-fishermen appear to have been artistically inferior to their predecessors. There are few ornaments, no mysterious batons, no carvings, no skeletons covered with red ochre. Their genius lay in composite instruments, in glue. Perhaps one can already observe the gulf between the 'two cultures', that of the sciences and that of the arts.

The Mesolithic Age lasted from about 10000 B.C. to about 3500 B.C. in the south. In northern areas it persisted much longer. Star Carr itself was occupied about 7500 B.C. This fairly precise date is obtained by the use of a very beautiful technique, known as the carbon 14 dating method. All living matter absorbs carbon 14, a radioactive substance, during its lifetime. After death the process ceases and the carbon 14 already absorbed begins, very slowly, to decay. By measuring the amount of carbon 14 still remaining in any organic specimen submitted for analysis, the scientific archaeologist can calculate how long ago the organic matter died. There is, of course, a margin of error. The Star Carr date would be given in full as 7538 ± 230 B.C., indicating a date somewhere between 7200 B.C. and 7900 B.C., with the probability that the correct date lies somewhere near the middle of that range. In this book the middle date will usually be given without adding the plus or minus range.

So far as Britain is concerned, the effect of carbon 14 dating has been to 'push back' many of the formerly accepted dates. Thus, not long ago it was believed that the New Stone Age in Britain dated from about the year 2500 B.C. Today its first appearance is placed 1,000 years earlier.

Carbon 14 dating can only be used for organic matter. It is because Mesolithic man used wood and because that wood has been preserved in peat and similar marsh deposits that such a site as Star Carr can be dated comparatively accurately.

Another valuable archaeological tool which can be used when analysing marshy deposits is that of pollen analysis. Pollen which falls onto the surface of water sinks to the bottom and is preserved in the mud or peat in successive layers. Borings taken can be analysed and the relative amount of different pollens can then be measured. This in turn provides an accurate record of the changing pattern of vegetation—and hence of the changes in climate which allowed a particular type of vegetation to take over. Such analysis shows that in England the countryside was dominated by forests of alder, elm, lime and oak as the warm and dry Boreal climate gave place to warm and damp conditions, known as Atlantic. About the middle of the fourth millenium the climate began to get drier again (Sub-Boreal). These dry, warm conditions lasted from about 3500 B.C. to about 1000 B.C.

II

THE NEW STONE AGE FARMERS:
3500 to 2000 B.C.

For about 6,000 years Mesolithic man had the land to himself.
Britain became a group of islands, and the Boreal gave place to the
Atlantic climate. Nevertheless in its essentials the inhabitants' way
of life changed little. Then, somewhere about 3500 B.C., startling
developments took place in southern Britain, developments that
had had their origins thousands of years earlier in the Near
East.

It was in the Fertile Crescent—the area that curves through
Iran, Iraq, Syria, southern Turkey, Israel and Egypt—that the
techniques of agriculture were first discovered. Somewhere in that
area, perhaps in southern Turkey, men learned, 10,000 years ago,
to supplement hunting by stock-raising, to supplement collecting
by cultivation. There grew the wild grasses which were the ancestors of barley and wheat, there roamed the wild animals that could
be domesticated.

From the Fertile Crescent the knowledge of these revolutionary
practices spread partly by trade, partly by migration, partly by
imitation. Great ripples of change moved slowly outwards towards
more distant, more backward, peoples, towards—finally—Britain.
By the time that these islands were adopting a primitive form of
pastoral farming, men in the Near East had taken the next step.
A surplus of food had made possible a civilization based on towns
and cities, a stable existence which brought with it writing and
the beginnings of history, as opposed to prehistory. These towns
are now known to be very much older than was formerly supposed.
Jericho was a walled town by 8000 B.C. Catal Hayuk in central

Turkey covered, in 6500 B.C., more than 30 acres. By the time Britain had adopted the first, agricultural Neolithic revolution, south-eastern Europe was already receiving this second, urban revolution. With the passing of time the ripples moved faster. It took 5,000 years for the Neolithic revolution to reach Britain, but it took only 1,000 years for the later Iron Age culture to arrive.

The knowledge of farming spread across Europe by three main routes: north over the plains of eastern Europe to the Baltic and Scandinavia; up the Danube valley and thence down the Rhine to the Low Countries; by way of the Mediterranean into southern France or through the straits of Gibraltar and thence up the coasts of Spain and Portugal.

All these routes led eventually to Britain. By 4000 B.C. farmers were established on the far side of the Channel. Within another 500 hundred years New Stone Age agriculturalists had reached Britain itself—the first invaders to come by sea across the relatively-recent English Channel. Before this time the land bridge and the ice cap had decided the areas of settlement; now the sea and the rivers, the soil and the hills, the headlands and the safe anchorages would control the pattern.

The land the Neolithic people reached had certain clearly-defined characteristics. Broadly speaking, the physical structure of Britain falls into two strongly contrasted parts. North and west of a line from Durham to Exeter the land is built of old, hard rocks. The terrain is mountainous, the soil often poor, the rainfall heavy. In contrast with this highland zone, the area to the south and east, the lowland zone, lies open to the continent. There are no ranges of hills more than a few hundred feet in height, the climate is drier, the soil—except in the Midlands—is easily worked. River valleys lead into the heart of the area.

A pattern of chalk or limestone ridges and upland areas, un-wooded or covered with vegetation that could be easily cleared, provided a ready-made system of roads. From the chalk plateau of Salisbury Plain and the White Horse Hills the chalk downs run south-west to the Dorset coast and east to the Kentish cliffs. The Chilterns run north-east from the same area and, changing their name to the Lincoln Wolds and the Yorkshire Wolds, reach the North Sea at Flamborough Head. A little to the north of these hills run the limestone Cotswolds, continued as Lincoln Edge and the Cleveland Hills and reaching the North Sea near Whitby. These lines of chalk and limestone provided the 'motorways' of prehistoric movement, with Salisbury Plain as their junction. This simple geological pattern explains a great deal in the distribution of settlement and the ease or otherwise with which cultural contacts between groups of settlers could be made.

In general the less accessible highland zone served primarily as an area of survival into which successive remnants from the lowland zone retreated in the face of new invasions from northwest Europe, but at certain times it acquired an importance of its own. Not all cultural contacts came by way of lowland Europe. Sometimes invaders and traders reached Britain by way of Spain and Brittany. They could find secure anchorages in the deeply indented western coasts and from thence could move north to Ireland and western Scotland. The hard rocks were suitable for the construction of tombs and the manufacture of stone implements, and in Cornwall, Ireland and Wales there were deposits of valuable minerals, tin, copper and gold.

Thus the two zones possessed contrasting advantages. Culture spread faster across the lowland zone, giving greater unity, but it survived longer in the highland zone, providing greater continuity. In the highland zone man had to fit himself into the existing pattern of mountains and valleys, while in the lowland zone he tended to impose himself on the landscape, even—as his technical equipment improved—altering that landscape to meet his demands and to support a growing population. The highland zone, by contrast, remained thinly populated, a source of raw materials rather than of agricultural developments.

The first Neolithic settlers must have reached the lowland zone by about 3500 B.C. As a result of migration from the north coast of France, settled agricultural communities were established along the Channel coast from Cornwall to Sussex. From these bases settlement had, comparatively soon, extended inland as far as the Vale of the White Horse (Berkshire/Oxfordshire).

In appearance the new men were small, lightly-boned, slender, with delicate hands and feet and long heads. (The ratio of the breadth of a skull to its length remains remarkably constant for different races. Archaeologists classify as 'long-headed', *dolichocephalic*, those in which the breadth is less than four-fifths of the length, as 'broad-headed', *brachycephalic*, those in which the breadth is four-fifths or more.)

These Neolithic settlers combined pastoral nomadism with hoe agriculture. That is to say, they herded their meat instead of hunting it, and they scratched around a little with primitive hoes and made corn plots. This involved a degree of permanent settlement, a regular return to base to look after the crop, a decision to remain in one area for at the very least a season or so. Nevertheless, for these primitive agriculturalists cattle-herding was more important than agriculture.

There is only a little evidence for a settled form of life, but at least two examples of timber-framed houses dating from this period have been discovered. The more instructive was at Haldon Hill to the south-west of Exeter. Here post-holes indicate a building about 20 feet long, 14½ feet wide at one end and 17 feet wide at the other, where the extra width served to accommodate the 'kitchen'—a basin-shaped depression of baked clay, about 5 feet in diameter. The post-holes and the cooking area were surrounded with stones which represent the remains of low walls above which once rose a wattle-and-daub framework sloping to a gabled roof. Picture a very low-walled thatched barn, its contours very uneven.

The way of life which developed from these first settlements is known as the Windmill Hill culture, from a site in north Wiltshire. Windmill Hill (SU/087714) lies to the west of road A361 (Swindon-Devizes). To reach it, leave the A361 by foot a mile north of Avebury. It was settled about 3000 B.C. and used by various peoples for 1,500 years. Finds from Windmill Hill are in the Avebury Museum.

Windmill Hill is an example of the most typical of the visible remains of the first Neolithic people, a causewayed camp. It is marked by three irregular ditches, approximately concentric and enclosing an area of about 23 acres. Although the site had been occupied some hundreds of years earlier, the existing ditches date from 2500 B.C. The outermost, deepest ditch was originally about eight feet deep, but weathering has reduced it by 2 or 3 feet. The ditches are interrupted by wide, irregularly-spaced gaps of undug ground which lead into the central area. It is this feature which is responsible for the name 'causewayed'. The banks of earth thrown up from the ditches were not high enough to act as defences and furthermore the wide causeways make nonsense of such an idea, even though there is evidence of the existence of some form of timber gateways.

What was the purpose of these camps, which clearly involved a great deal of co-ordinated effort? The answer, almost certainly, has been found in the ditches. There have been unearthed large quantities of bones belonging to the animals domesticated by the Neolithic people, animals such as goats, sheep, small pigs and small, long-horned oxen. The oxen have often been pole-axed over the right eye and many of the bones show scratches where the flesh was removed by the flint scrapers which still lay with the bones when they were unearthed.

These finds suggest the slaughter of animals in the autumn, and the use of the camps as seasonal enclosures where the animals could be corralled while the feast and cattle-fair was in full swing. The herdsmen and their families camped in the ditches, presumably in rough tents, where the remains of hearths have been found.

Two sets of bones are of particular interest. A dwarf had been buried in the outer ditch soon after it was dug. And, elsewhere, there was found the skeleton of a dog, long-legged and short-backed, standing about 16 inches high, the oldest domesticated dog in Britain.

In earlier periods one is concerned with natural features such as caves, or with the barest scrapings of earth so scattered and cautious that today there is usually nothing for the untrained eye to see. Now man begins to alter the landscape, a process that has continued ever since. Even apparently 'natural' landscapes have been modelled by man as he fenced and ditched, burnt and cleared.

From the traveller's point of view the supply of visible sites increases rapidly and he can pick and choose from the wealth of examples which to visit and which to leave for another time. There are more than a dozen causewayed camps which might be visited. Windmill Hill has many advantages. Important in itself, it is close to other interesting sites. The museum which houses the finds is at hand. Further, it is a pleasant site in itself. The eighteenth-century archaeologist, William Stukeley called it "a very delicate hill" and remarked on "the turf as soft as velvet". A man of sensibility.

As a second choice I would make for a very different place, Hembury in South Devon. Hembury (SX/726684) lies on the north side of road A373 (Honiton-Cullompton) about 4 miles out of Honiton. Finds are in the Exeter Museum.

Hembury is an Iron Age hill-fort, but within its boundaries, constructed 3,000 years earlier, there lies a Neolithic causewayed camp, occupied before Windmill Hill, about 3200 B.C. Visiting Hembury one gets, as it were, two for the price of one. Climb the steep path from the road and one passes first through Iron Age banks and ditches with a V-shaped profile. Continue northwards and one reaches eight lengths of ditch with gaps between them and a U-shaped profile. These were made to cut off the end of the spur along which one has just walked. This difference in profile is a convenient way of distinguishing Neolithic from Iron Age camps. Continue walking northwards and one comes to the great Iron Age ramparts which defended the flat northern end of the camp.

The Neolithic people lived at the tip of the spur and just outside the north-western end of their ramparts. They also had some sort of timber gatehouse controlling the western entrance. These features are another reason for visiting Hembury. Normally cause-wayed camps did not contain permanent settlements.

Hembury, on greensand, has still plenty of trees around it. Standing on a downland site, such as Windmill Hill, one may be led astray by the bare contours. Although chalk and limestone always carried a much lighter vegetation than the damp clay low-lands, it is nevertheless pretty certain that they were originally wooded and that they were cleared, partially or completely, quite early in the Neolithic occupation.

The land cleared, crops could be grown. At Hembury stone grain-rubbers (saddle-querns) have been found. Carbonised grain, to-gether with the impressions left by individual grains in the clay of neolithic pottery provide evidence as to what sort of crops were cultivated. About 90 per cent of the total consists of two sorts of wheat—emmer and small wheat—while the remainder is barley.

The pottery in which these impressions of grain have been found is one of the most significant developments in the Neolithic 'break-through'. Previously men had used gourds, wattle baskets lined with clay, or leather bags as containers. There is a famous draw-ing of a Mesolithic man collecting wild honey in what is quite clearly a bag. The stock-raising Neolithic people had a particular need for reliable containers both for grain and milk.

The first baked clay vessels were not thrown on a wheel, but were coil-pots. A long sausage of clay was rolled between the palms and then built up into the required shape, the corrugations being smoothed out. The earliest Windmill Hill pottery is pretty rough-looking, round-bottomed, bag-shaped stuff, with a maxi-mum diameter of about 6 inches. Later pottery became a little smarter, imitating closely the shape of the leather bucket from which it was derived. These buckets had had their rim stitched over a wooden hoop to keep the mouth open, and the clay imita-tion extends to the stitching itself, represented by a pattern of short parallel lines, or rows of dots, scratched round the neck or shoulder of the pot.

In the Near East the secret of fired pottery was not discovered until long after the beginnings of agriculture. By the time the changed way of life had reached Britain there was little or no time gap between the two developments.

Pottery may be regarded, from the technical point of view, as the first example of applied chemistry (unless we extend this category to include the discovery of fire itself, an isolated event which took place early in the Old Stone Age). The firing of clay was the first occasion when men deliberately changed the chemical structure of a substance to satisfy their needs.

Pottery has an especial value to the archaeologist. All primitive crafts—flint-knapping, potting, metal-working—are rigidly bound by conservatism and convention. The craft is often secret, and only one way is the 'right' way to make things. Hence the exact construction and patterning of a pot becomes a valuable indicator of connections between widely separated groups, a clue through the labyrinth of increasingly complex cultural groupings in Europe.

Neolithic people continued to use flaked flints for many purposes. Indeed, a willow-leaf shaped arrowhead, about 2 inches long, is a characteristic implement widely distributed in eastern and southern England. They also, however, developed a new technique, that of grinding and polishing flint and stone, particularly for use as axe-heads—smooth and lovely objects about 6 inches long. The idea may have come from watching the action of the stone rubbers as grain was ground into flour between them. Mechanically, it was an important step forward. Neolithic man was a great clearer of light timber. Modern experiments have shown that, using the old-fashioned flaked flint axe, it takes about seven minutes to chop down a tree 7 inches in diameter but that the same work can be done in only five minutes with a polished blade.

A further advantage of using polished stone was that flint ceased to be the most satisfactory raw material. Many hard crystalline rocks were suitable material on which to employ the new technique. They were found in the highland zone, where flint was conspicuous by its absence. Trade routes were opened up as the new axes were brought to the lowland zone from sources of supply as far apart as Cornwall (Penzance), North Wales (Graig Lwyd), the Lake District (Langdale Pike) and even northern Ireland (Cushendall). The use of these sources developed soon after 3000 B.C., became a dominant feature perhaps about 2500 B.C.

and continued into the second millenium. By that time other groups had replaced the original Neolithic settlers, but the trade went on. A rather special feature was the introduction of a few ceremonial axe-heads of jadeite from Brittany (Morbihan).

Side by side with the development outlined above, flint-mining continued to flourish. Flint was still used in the lowland areas, it was also part of a two-way trade with the highland zone. Indeed the peak of flint-mining may have been as late as 2000 B.C.

There is clear evidence that in some areas mining became a specialized occupation. Mines are known at Martin's Clump near Salisbury where over 100 pits have been found, at Peppard on the Chilterns in Oxfordshire, in Sussex at Cissbury where over 200 pits have been identified, and at Stoke Down near Chichester. At Peppard the flint occurred close to the surface of the ground and could be mined by what might be termed 'open-cast working', but surface flints flaked badly and flint mines were usually in the form of shafts. At Harrow Hill in Sussex such shafts were sunk, but the soil has fallen in over the centuries and now there is nothing to see but unimpressive hollows.

At Grime's Graves in Norfolk, by contrast, 3 acres of workings have been cleared and can be visited. This is one of the great pre-historic sites from the traveller's point of view.

Grime's Graves (TL/817898) can be reached by taking road A1065 (Brandon-Swaffham) out of Brandon and forking right along road B1108. The mines are less than a mile to the south of the A134/B1108 crossroads. Two shafts are open for inspection, there is a small museum on the site, and there are finds in the museums at Norwich and Thetford, close by.

The mines indicate remarkable technical skill and considerable physical effort on the part of the miners. There must have been a strong demand for flint—a seller's market. The shafts sink 30 to 40 feet through useless sand, boulder-clay and chalk, past layers of low-grade flint, until they reach the miners' goal, the layer of best quality 'floorstone'. The diameter of the shafts is much the same as their depth, varying between 28 and 42 feet. At the bottom of the shaft low galleries 2 or 3 feet high run in all direc-tions, linking up eventually after perhaps 30 or 40 feet with galleries from other shafts. As in the early days of coal-mining, the roof was supported by leaving large pillars of uncut rock and the spoil from a gallery in use would be dumped in one that was exhausted. This made for stability and also saved the unnecessary work of carrying waste material to ground level, for there were

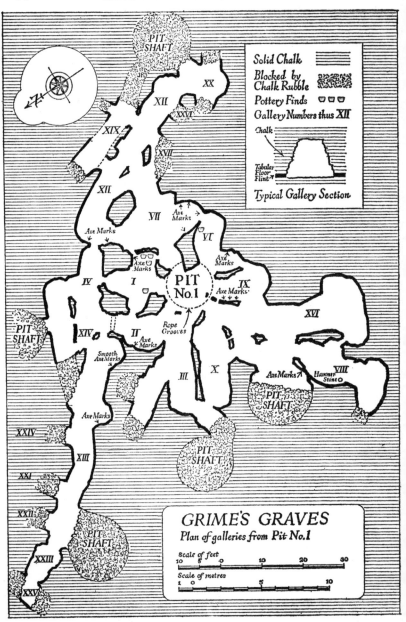

N

Solid Chalk

**Blocked by
Chalk Rubble**

Pottery Finds

Gallery Numbers thus XII

Chalk

Tabular
Floor
Flint

Typical Gallery Section

PIT
SHAFT

XX

XII

XXVI

XIX

XVII

XII

VII

Axe
Marks

Axe Marks

VI

Axe
Marks

Axe
Marks

IV

I

**PIT
No.1**

IX

Axe Marks

XVI

PIT
SHAFT

XIV

II

Axe
Marks

Rope
Grooves

Smooth
Axe Marks

III

X

Axe Marks

Hammer
Stone

VIII

PIT
SHAFT

XXIV

Axe Marks

XIII

PIT
SHAFT

XXI

XXII

PIT
SHAFT

XXIII

XXV

GRIME'S GRAVES
Plan of galleries from Pit No.1

Scale of feet
10   5   0   10   20   30

Scale of metres
1   0   5   10

(Reproduced by permission of the Ministry of Public Building and Works)

no steps in these mines—everything had to be hauled to the surface.

Specialized equipment was needed for the mining operations. At Grime's Graves the miners used the antlers of red deer, trimmed so that only the brow tine was left as a pick. These were probably held in the left hand, the antler tip to a weak point, and then hammered behind the brow tine, for there are signs of wear at this point on the broken antlers that have been found still lying where they were discarded in the galleries. On the shafts of some of these picks there is a most evocative pattern in the chalk caked on the antler shaft, a pattern which is made up of the finger-prints of Neolithic miners, a finger-print collection 4,000 years old.

There are other signs to remind one that living men once moved along these galleries, signs less personal than the finger-prints, but that provide important clues to the organization of the mine. In some of the galleries there are sets of scratches. These probably represent the record of loads taken out, or of days worked. At Harrow Hill the soot from the miners' lamps had marked the roof of the workings. The lamps would have been little open wells of clay, or perhaps of the chalk itself, in which a wick floated in a pool of animal fat.

Besides the antler picks the miners used stone axes and shovels made from the shoulder-blades of oxen. The material was taken to the surface in baskets or leather buckets by means of ropes or thongs slung over beams at the top of the shaft—the marks made by the rubbing of the ropes and the sockets for the beams can still be seen. The miners must themselves have climbed up and down these ropes, or they may perhaps have used notched logs as ladders.

Once at ground level the raw material was manufactured, or partly manufactured. The flint was split, the approximate shape roughed out, the exact shape flaked. Grinding and polishing was apparently not undertaken on the site. These processes seem to have been carried out by the purchaser, or by travelling middlemen.

Here, clearly, was a society of craftsmen producing a particular commodity to be distributed and exchanged over a wide area. The self-sufficiency of the family group has already begun to be eroded —a process that leads without a break to the complex international structure of modern society. The Neolithic demand for stone and flint was, at least in part, satisfied by this comparatively complex structure of mining communities and trade routes.

The materials available to Neolithic man included not only flint and stone, but also bone and wood. It is probable that his clothes were of leather. Large bone combs have been recovered which were clearly not intended for human hair, but rather for dealing with animal skins. The antlers of red deer were used for hoes and picks, and the resulting crops were harvested with flint sickles. The bow and arrow played an important part. Reference has already been made to the leaf-shaped arrow-heads, angular heads later evolved into a very sophisticated tanged shape.

In general, wood has not survived, but an axe with beechwood shaft has been recovered from a tarn in Cumberland and two bows have been found in the Somerset Levels, where the wet marshes had preserved them. Their date is about 2700 B.C. They are of yew, 5 feet long, and they bear a close resemblance to the medieval longbow that became the Englishman's 'secret weapon' in the Hundred Years' War with France. Then the English had adopted the longbow from the Welsh when they conquered Wales—and it was to the Welsh highland zone that prehistoric peoples were driven by later waves of invaders. In the light of these facts it is not unreasonable to see in the longbow of Crecy and Agincourt the descendant of a Neolithic weapon in use 4,000 years before.

On the Somerset Levels, too, timber trackways have been discovered in the peat. These tracks, 2 to 5 feet wide, consist of a birch and hazel framework with brushwood laid across it. Radio carbon dating places them within the period 2350 to 2100 B.C.

Neolithic man had spiritual, as well as material, concerns. In one of the shafts of the flint mines at Grime's Graves, resting on a little ledge, there was found the chalk-cut figure of a pregnant woman. Below lay a chalk phallus and a pile of antler picks. Significantly, this particular shaft had not reached workable flint, it was sterile, unproductive. The link between the objects placed there and the barren pit is clear. This clumsy little fertility shrine throws a clear light through the darkness onto the religious beliefs of the men who sank that useless shaft.

There are other indications, more widespread if less unambiguous, of another aspect of religion, a belief in the individual afterlife. From the earliest Neolithic times there exist here and there little lonely graves, scratchings in the ground, their loneliness qualified only by the existence of a clay pot, which once held food or drink for the comfort or necessity of the dead. (Against this concern for the dead one must remember to set the discovery of a grisly mixture of human and animal bones found in the ditches of some of the causewayed camps, remains which point clearly to the eating of human flesh.)

The ordinary people might be buried with little ceremony or eaten with even less, but some families—and one must suppose that they were those that possessed religious and political authority, either separately or in combination—obtained a very different and highly imposing end in the long barrows which are still such a conspicuous feature of the southern downlands.

There are something between 150 and 200 long barrows of one sort or another still visible in Wessex alone. The earliest type, and the most general in that area, is the earthen long barrow. 'Earthen' is in this context a general term, the barrows may be composed of chalk, soil, or in suitable areas, quite small stones.

These barrows are marked by flanking ditches from which the material was dug to raise them. The majority range in length from 40 to 400 feet, in width from 30 to 140 feet, and in present height from just above ground level to about 10 feet. Carefully sited, a long barrow of shining white chalk was both a monument creating pride and a tomb inspiring awe.

Three exceptionally long barrows occur in Dorset: Came Wood (SY/695855) is 600 feet long; Long Barrow Hill (SY/572912) is 645 feet in length; while at Maiden Castle (SY/668885) there is a giant measuring 1,790 feet. These bank barrows are regarded as late, insular developments, perhaps related to the cursus (see pp. 60–1). Long Barrow Hill lies south of road A35 (Bridport–Dorchester) close to the minor road leading to Long Bredy.

In spite of the variation in size, the excavation of a large number of long barrows has provided something of a common pattern. Usually there are pits in the floor of the barrow; above these and extending the whole length of the mound is a spine of decayed turf, humus or—exceptionally—stones; over this is the enclosing material dug from the flanking ditches. The final tomb is usually wider and higher at one end, and is often orientated east-west; when this is the case, the higher end is usually the eastern one.

In comparison with the size of a barrow, the tomb equipment was on a very limited scale—a few flints, a pot or two, perhaps the horns of an ox—nothing more. On the floor and typically at the higher end are the burials. Normally anything up to twenty to thirty individuals were buried in these communal graves, the bones of people of all ages and both sexes heaped indiscriminately.

The explanation for this rather odd arrangement is thought to be roughly as follows. The bodies of the dead were accumulated, until the critical moment arrived, in irregular wooden mortuary houses, or in earthern enclosures, the wooden type being something like the long houses of New Guinea. When the flesh had perished and the skeletons were naturally disarticulated, all were buried at one time. Sometimes the final mound was built over the mortuary house, which was burnt before raising the mound, but for many barrows there is no evidence of a mortuary house. Thus the earthern long barrow was a communal, once for all, tomb.

So much is clear. The unanswered question is—when did the ceremony take place? After the direct family line had ended? After a whole generation had died? When the heavens seemed propitious? The answer is not likely to be recovered.

The first discovery of a wooden mortuary house was made by General Pitt-Rivers at Wor Barrow in Dorset. It was a complete excavation in the General's best manner and the mound was completely cleared. Today one sees only the excavated ditch and an empty space within. In spite of—or perhaps because of—this, it is worth visiting as a classic site. Wor Barrow (SU/012173) lies on the north side of road A354 (Blandford Forum-Salisbury) 11 miles from Blandford and a little north of the point at which the road B3081 crosses the main road. The finds from Wor Barrow are in the Pitt-Rivers Museum at nearby Farnham.

The excavations disclosed the remains of a rectangular wooden enclosure 90 by 35 feet, surrounded by a ditch 140 by 90 feet. Later a second ditch—the one that can now be seen—was dug and it was the material from this ditch that was used to cover the enclosure with a mound. Six bodies were found, three of which were no more than loose skeletons when buried.

When Wor Barrow was excavated the wooden building was thought to be unique. Since then similar structures have been found associated with other barrows, including Fussel's Lodge near Salisbury and Nutbane near Andover. At Normanton Down (SU/115413) which lies close to the field track (SU/114411) running south from A303 at Stonehenge, the mortuary enclosure was outside the barrow and just to the south. It is said that under favourable conditions—that is, with the help of the long shadows of sunrise or sunset—the outline can still be seen.

From southern England the practice of erecting these earthen long barrows spread northwards, together with other features of the Windmill Hill culture, along the chalk and limestone routes to Lincolnshire and the East and North Ridings of Yorkshire. The process was slow and in the farther north the barrows were in general being constructed 500 years or more after those in the south.

In Lincolnshire at Giants Hills (TF/429712) three-quarters of a mile north-west of Skendleby—turn west off road A1028 (Skegness-Louth)—a long barrow lies on ploughland, but still shows up. Here a rectangular wooden mortuary house 189 by 37 feet had been built. On a chalk platform there were the remains of eight people. Three sets of bones were weathered and in one of the skulls there was a snail's egg-case of a type only found in the open air. Clearly at least three of the bodies had been 'stored' in such a way that they were exposed to the elements for a considerable time. Finds are in the British Museum.

Farther north, Willerby Wold (TA/029761) is in the East Riding of Yorkshire. It lies 2 miles south of Staxton, a village on road A64 (York-Scarborough). Follow road B1249 south and then turn left along the minor road signposted Fordon for one mile. Willerby Wold is then on your right just to the south of the road. Finds are in the British Museum.

At the wider end of Willerby Wold the loose bones had been placed on the ground. They had been covered with a carefully constructed stack of chalk, flint and wood. This funeral pyre was then set alight. The bones were cremated and the chalk reduced to lime—in fact, the whole structure worked like a lime kiln. This crematorium is not unique, but it seems to have been a very localized practice. So far eight have been discovered. Seven of these are in Yorkshire and one in the neighbouring county of Westmorland.

There has only been space to mention a few of the great number of earthen long barrows still in existence. Amongst others worth visiting are those in the list, a purely personal choice of 'seven for the road'.

Berkshire: Combe Gibbett (SU/365263), west of A343 (Andover-Newbury).

Dorset: Pimperne (ST/917104), north of A354 (Blandford-Salisbury).

Hampshire: Danebury (SU/320383), south of A343 (Salisbury-Andover).

Hertfordshire: Therfield Heath (TL/342402), west of A10 (Royston-Ware).

Kent: Julliberrie's Grave (TR/077532), south of A252 (Canterbury-Charing).

Lincolnshire: Hoe Hill (TF/215953), west of B1203 (Market Rasen-Grimsby).

Norfolk: West Rudham (TF/810254), south of A148 (King's Lynn-Fakenham).

III

MEGALITHIC MONUMENTS:

2700 to 1700 B.C.

These earthen long barrows, though well worth visiting, are not the most dramatic form of Neolithic burial mound. Pride of place must undoubtedly be given to the chambered tomb—consisting of a mound, long or round, enclosing a stone chamber or chambers, a type found mainly to the west and north of the long barrows just described, dominating the highland zone and adjoining areas.

At some date in the third millenium, probably about 2700 B.C. or a little earlier, invasion by way of the sea-route up the western coasts of Britain introduced a culture related to the Windmill Hill type, but differing from it in certain important respects.

The area affected was much greater. It included Cornwall, the Cotswolds, Wales, Ireland, the Isle of Man, the Lake District, and western and northern Scotland. It was probably the first time that this area had received its culture directly, and not indirectly from lowland zone migrants.

The ancestry of the stone tombs is thought to be as follows. In the Mediterranean area communal tombs carved out of the rock were a typical feature of the New Stone Age. In western Europe, in southern France and in parts of Spain these rock-cut tombs were replaced by a stone version built at ground level, using large stone uprights, and covered with a mound of earth—an artificial cave. There were also constructed large stone (megalithic) monuments of other types. In addition to chambered tombs the main forms are single standing stones, stone rows, and stone circles. It has been estimated that, taking all types into account, there are more than 40,000 megalithic monuments still standing in western Europe alone.

Within the British Isles there are about 2,000 megalithic tombs. The distribution of these is significant: there are about 1,000 in Ireland, 350 in Scotland, and perhaps 250 in England, of which something approaching a quarter are in the Isles of Scilly. Without considering any other evidence, these figures lead to the conclusion that the vast majority of megalithic builders reached Britain by the western sea-route mentioned above. (There is a small isolated group of barrows in south-east England, of which Kit's Coty House (see p. 49) is the best-known example. These, it is assumed, were erected by builders who had penetrated up the Channel and crossed to Kent from north-east France or Holland.)

A considerable amount of space and energy has been devoted by professionals to the drawing-up of various schemes of classification for chambered tombs. No neat, generally accepted system has emerged. So far as the ordinary traveller is concerned, a rough and ready pattern to carry in one's mind is as follows. There are two small specialized groups, the Kentish one already referred to, and one based on the Isles of Scilly and western Cornwall, consisting of entrance graves and Penwith tombs (see p. 50). The two main groups, widely distributed, are known as gallery graves and passage graves. In the former, burials occur in small compartments on either side of a central corridor covered by a long mound; in the latter a stone-lined passage leads to a single vault, covered by a round mound.

What was the relationship between these different types? It seems probable that the religious drive behind the erection of all must have possessed many common features, but it seems equally clear that the ritual details varied considerably. A comparison has been made with Christian buildings. All derive from a common faith, but the differences between the construction and internal arrangements of, on the one hand a 'tin chapel' and, on the other, a Gothic cathedral, are so great that an archaeologist would be hard put to it to deduce the common faith from the two buildings. Or consider the part played respectively by the High Altar of St. Peter's, the stone altar of an English village church, and the wooden table of a Nonconformist chapel—all similar in general ground plan.

Gallery graves are the most common in England and Wales. They appear to have orginated in western France in the region of the Loire and southern Brittany. They are thick on the ground in the Severn-Cotswold region, but they are also found in Ulster-Clyde-Solway, and some consider these as a single Clyde-Severn group.

The English and Welsh gallery graves were built by small groups of immigrants who sailed up the Bristol Channel and settled the coasts on either side, landing in Gower and at the western end of the Cotswolds, and eventually colonizing the Brecknockshire Black Mountains, the Gloucestershire Cotswolds, the area around Windmill Hill, and the eastern end of the Mendips. They appear to have created peaceably a hybrid culture with the existing inhabitants whether these were, as in South Wales, at the Mesolithic stage, or, as at Windmill Hill, in a more advanced stage of development.

The Severn-Cotswold gallery graves are in general easy of access and dramatic in appearance. Many are worth visiting. Once again there is great variation in size. A good average would be between 100 and 200 feet in length, 10 feet in height, 50 feet wide at one end and about 30 at the other, the whole construction being like a pear sliced lengthways. The wider end is thus the highest point and here, orginally, was the entrance, often walled up and partially enclosed by two curving horns of dry-stone walling which created a sort of forecourt. Here it is proposed to describe five of the best-known examples.

Opposite Silbury Hill on the south side of road A4 (Marlborough-Chippenham) lies West Kennet (SU/104677). Finds are in the museum at Devizes, 6 miles to the south. West Kennet, 350 feet long and 75 feet wide, is one of the largest long barrows in England and Wales. It was probably built about 2700 B.C.

A core of sarsen (sandstone) boulders is covered with a mound of chalk dug from ditches running parallel to the long sides of the barrow. At one time there was a kerb of stones round the outside of the mound, but this has now gone. Within the barrow a gallery almost 8 feet high runs for about 40 feet. There is an end chamber and two pairs of side chambers—five in all. On some of the internal uprights patches of polishing can still be seen. (Look at the north face of the upright separating the second chamber on the left (SW) from the gallery.) These are places where axe-heads were ground sharp during the construction of the barrow. The axes would be used to cut timber scaffolding employed in the erection of the stones.

At least forty-six people had been buried in the chambers, the burials extending over a very long period of time. Since more jaw-

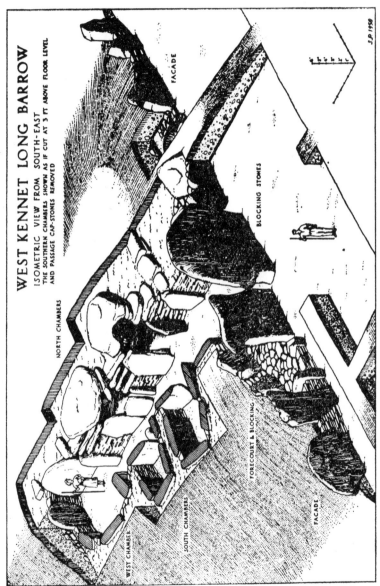

WEST KENNET LONG BARROW

ISOMETRIC VIEW FROM SOUTH-EAST
THE SOUTHERN CHAMBERS SHOWN AS IF CUT AT 3 FT ABOVE FLOOR LEVEL
AND PASSAGE CAP-STONES REMOVED

FACADE

NORTH CHAMBERS

BLOCKING STONES

WEST CHAMBER

SOUTH CHAMBERS

FORECOURT & BLOCKING

FACADE

S.P. 1958

(Reproduced by permission of the Ministry of Public Building and Works)

bones than skulls have been found, it is assumed that the skulls were used for religious purposes. A number of thighbones are also missing. Sufficient remains have been found, however, for one to say that the people buried there had good teeth, often suffered from arthritis, and were much the same height as today—the women average 5 feet 4 inches, the men 5 feet 8 inches.

Eventually the barrow was finally closed. The passages and chambers were filled up with fresh chalk rubble, and the entrance blocked with large stones—one huge block weighs 50 tons. The gaps were closed with dry-stone walling, the stones coming from 8 to 12 miles away, in the neighbourhood of Calne. This front—which is what one sees today—was put up about 1,800 B.C. or perhaps even later, probably by Beaker people (see p. 72). It hides the original façade, which was concave, enclosing a semi-circular forecourt presumably used for ritual purposes.

A fine specimen is at Stony Littleton (ST/735572) in Somerset, 3 miles north-east of Radstock. Take road A367 (Radstock-Bath). Turn south from the main road 2 miles out of Radstock and follow the minor road towards Wellow. Turn right at the second cross-roads for Stoney Littleton. Ask for permission at Stoney Littleton Farm. Finds are in the Bristol City Museum.

The barrow is 107 feet long and 54 feet wide, with a maximum height of 10 feet, and aligned north-west/south-east. There is a forecourt at the south-eastern end, a chamber just inside, and then a 40-foot passage with six paired side-chambers. The walls are constructed of large stones, with dry-stone walling filling the gaps. The roof is corbelled, roughly but skilfully. On one of the uprights at the entrance there is the fossilised pattern of an ammonite. Many prehistoric structures are ornamented with man-made spirals and this apparently magical carving already in existence must have endowed the stone in which it was found with great rarity and potency.

In the heart of the Cotswolds there are several imposing gallery graves. Two of the most impressive are the charmingly named Hetty Pegler's Tump and Belas Knap, both in Gloucestershire. Less than 30 miles apart they can be visited and compared in one afternoon.

Hetty Pegler's Tump (SO/789001) is the more dramatic. Take road A38 (Bristol-Gloucester) and about half-way along it turn off by road A4135 to Dursley. At Dursley fork left along B4066 to Uley. The barrow lies one mile beyond Uley Church. You will need the key from Mr. Parsloe, Frocester Hill Filling Station, Nympsfield, a few miles further on, and you should take a torch or, better still, a candle.

The Tump is 120 feet by 85 feet at its eastern end. It resembles West Kennet fairly closely, but here the gallery is still roofed in. There is a forecourt, two pairs of side chambers, and a fifth chamber at the end of the gallery. Only the pair of chambers on the south side is still accessible. When the barrow was opened in 1854 fifteen skeletons were found. (Fifteen, incidentally, is the average number from twenty-four Cotswold barrows opened.) The flickering light of the candle provides a suitably atmospheric lighting. Blow it out and feel the ancient back-to-the-womb darkness close in around you before it opens out again as your eyes become accustomed to the half-light.

To reach Belas Knap (SP/022254) take road A46 (Cheltenham-Stratford). At Winchcombe, 6 miles from Cheltenham, turn onto B4078 which leads to Charlton Abbas. Belas Knap lies to the right of this road, about 2 miles out of Winchcombe. Finds are in the museum at Cheltenham.

Belas Knap is a late barrow, built about 2000 B.C., less numinous than Hetty Pegler's Tump, but with some special features. At first sight it appears normal except for the fact that it lies north and south. It is 174 feet by 60 wide at its northern end. There is a very impressive forecourt, leading to a doorway blocked by another large stone and some dry-stone walling.

The difference is that, here, this elaborate construction is a fraud. There is not, and there never has been, a way into Belas Knap from the forecourt. The mound is solid, built of lumps of limestone held in place by a low stone wall—the stones of the existing retaining wall are a modern restoration. In the outside face of the barrow four burial chambers were constructed, each entered by a short passage, two on the east side, one on the west and one at the southern end.

The remains of at least thirty-eight people have been found in these chambers. A significant number of skulls showed signs of having received a blow a little before or a little after the time of death. Were their owners sacrificed? Was a primitive form of euthanasia practised? Were the blows designed to release the spirit? Or to prevent the dead from rising again and plaguing the living? The bones do not reply.

And what about the false entrance? Belas Knap is not by any means the only long barrow with this feature. Opinion is divided as to the purpose of these false entrances. Some believe they were

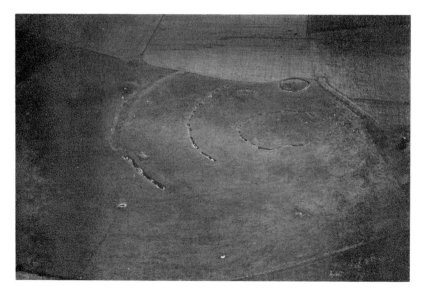

Windmill Hill, Neolithic causewayed camp. Only part of the three ditches has been left open after excavation. A string of Bronze Age round barrows can be seen in the middle distance.

Grimes Graves, prehistoric flint mine. Galleries radiate from a central shaft. The black patches are inferior flint passed over by the miners.

West Kennet, Neolithic long barrow. The kerb of sarsens *(above)* and the central passage *(left)*.

designed to frustrate tomb robbers, as in Egypt. Others think that the false doorway was designed to mislead, not robbers from the world of the living, but spirits from the land of the dead.

A third explanation, perhaps the most likely is that the forecourt served a ritual purpose, not only at funeral times but perhaps also at other great festivals. If that were so, it would be necessary to construct it, even though the entrances to the burial chambers were elsewhere. Religious architecture is littered with obsolescent features of a similar kind.

The fifth chambered tomb is Wayland's Smithy, lying gaunt and exposed in its circle of trees to the north of a prehistoric ridgeway. The Smithy (SU/281854) can be reached by following road B4507 (Swindon-Wantage) and turning south at the appropriate Ministry of Works sign. It can be conveniently combined with visits to Uffington Castle and the White Horse (Iron Age; see pp. 141, 156). The barrow is 185 feet by 43 feet and contains three chambers, a pair and a singleton at the end of the gallery. It overlies an earlier construction of which nothing is really visible. The great stones that face one as one approaches are the re-erected facing. Beyond are the chambers. The right-hand (southern) one still has its capstone. It was on this stone that later travellers might leave a groat, their horse tethered close by. Returning in the morning, they would find their groat gone and their horse shod by the legendary Wayland. The story is at least as early as the tenth century (A.D. 955) and who knows how much older? Wayland, a figure of Scandinavian mythology, owned a white horse, which may account for his name becoming attached to this particular tomb, but the awe in which metal-workers were held is very much older than that.

Chambered tombs in other parts of England which are worth a visit include:

Cheshire: Bridestones (SJ/906622), east of A527 (Stoke-Congleton).
Dorset: Grey Mare and Her Colts (SY/583871), north of B3157 (Bridport-Weymouth).
Herefordshire: Arthur's Stone (SO/318431), north of B4349 (Hay-Hereford).
Kent: Kit's Coty House (TQ/745608), west of A229 (Maidstone-Rochester).
Oxfordshire: Whispering Knights (SP/299308), west of A34 (Oxford-Stratford).

The second major type, the passage grave, is rare in England and Wales, though common in Ireland and Scotland. The examples

D

found in England and Wales were either erected by passage-grave migrants on their way north, or the pattern reached the mainland as a result of diffusion from Ireland itself. Contact between their builders and other groups seem to have resulted in the development of hybrids, notably in Cornwall, and the Isles of Scilly, an area well provided with megalithic tombs.

A detailed analysis of these south-western examples can be found in Lady Aileen Fox's *South West England*. Here there is only room for an outline.

Lady Fox divides south-western chambered tombs into four groups. There are gallery graves, mainly in the east of the county, of the Severn-Cotswold type. Of these, the partly exposed example of Pawton (SW/968683) on St. Breock Downs south-west of Wadebridge, is worth a visit.

The second group, Penwith tombs, are constructed of a circular cairn, 30 feet or so in diameter, covering a small square stone chamber. They are concentrated in the Land's End area and are late in date, probably as late as 1600 B.C. Zennor Quoit (SW/469380) is a good example of this intermediate type, although the magnificent 18-foot capstone now rests partly on the ground because a farmer saw fit to take away supporting stones to build a cow-shed. The remains indicate a chamber and an ante-chamber, separated by a stone barrier. The Quoit lies one mile south of Zennor and quite close to the road on the south side. Finds are in Truro Museum.

Lady Fox's third group consists of one true passage grave at Broadsands near Paignton in Devon. It is archaeologically interesting because of its singularity, but the traveller will find more excitement in the fourth group—entrance graves, which are derived from the passage grave family, but in which there is no passage, the chamber being entered from the edge of the mound, which is itself about 20 feet in diameter and kerbed with stones. The entrance graves are found in the Land's End peninsula and in the Isles of Scilly, which is thought to have been their original base. A dramatic example, though not perhaps a typical one, is the grave at Carn Gluze (SW/355313) which has a very complicated history. It lies one mile west of St. Just on the cape. Less exciting, but more typical is the grave at Pennance (SW/448376) about one mile south-west of Zennor.

The enthusiast can spend a lifetime specializing in Cornish variants, just as the keen philatelist may devote his life to penny red overseas postmarks. Other fairly well-preserved specimens of various types are Brane (SW/401282), Chun Quoit (SW/402340), Mulfra Quoit (SW/452354) and Treen (SW/402340).

The pattern of chambered tombs in Wales is interesting. One of the difficulties of writing about 'prehistoric England' is that one is dealing with an artificial political division. Cornwall is clearly part of the highland zone, as are some parts of northern England. Conversely, south-east Wales was usually tied in to the lowland zone, while south-west Wales and parts of the north more often than not received their cultural influences from Ireland.

Thus in south-east Wales the chambered tombs are gallery graves in the Severn-Cotswold tradition. Good examples can be seen at Tinkinswood (ST/092733) south of A38 (Cowbridge-Cardiff) about 6 miles from Cardiff; Maen Ceti on the Gower peninsula (SS/491905) north of road A4118 (Port Eynon-Swansea) near Reynoldstown, with a monster capstone weighing 25 tons and said to have been thrown there by King Arthur, who found it in his shoe; and Ty Isaf (SO/182291) close to A479 (Abergavenny-Talgarth).

In south-west Wales the tomb at Pentre Ifan, (SN/099370) north of B4329 (Haverfordwest-Cardigan) about 8 miles from Cardigan, is thought to have been the product of Irish influence. Today it is a highly dramatic huddle of stones.

In northern Wales there are once again indications of Severn-Cotswold influence at Capel Garmon (SH/818544) to the east of A5 (Pentre Foelas-Llanwrist). In this area, though, the interest lies in the two true passage graves, directly connected with Ireland and both situated on Anglesey: Barclodiad y Gawres (SH/328708) and Bryn Celli Ddu (SH/508702).

Barclodiad lies at the end of the track from Porth Trecastell. It has been heavily restored, but expertly and recently. What one sees is a passage grave with a cross-shaped burial chamber. Notice particularly the carvings on five of the stones, very similar to those in Ireland at, for instance, New Grange (see below, p. 52) and very rare on the mainland. Placed on the route by which Irish gold and copper passed to continental Europe, it is hardly a coincidence that the grave overlooks a good natural harbour.

On the central hearth ashes were found and have been analysed. They include the remains of whiting, eels, frogs, toads and snakes, mice, shrews and hare which had been boiled together. Under the hearth was found part of a pig. The whole suggests deep magic rather than poor food.

Bryn Celli Ddu lies south of road A5 (Menai-Holyhead). Take

the southern turning to Llanddaniel Fab about 4 miles out of Menai. Just to the south, follow the farm road to the farm and ask for the key. Like Barclodiad, Bryn has close connections with Ireland. Originally there was a large mound about 160 feet in diameter, which covers stone circles, a pillar stone, a 20-foot passage and a D-shaped chamber. Much of this has now disappeared and what one can see is the mound over the passage and chamber. Sections of the circles can be picked out on the open ground. A carved stone is now in the Welsh National Museum, but a cast stands on the site. Beneath it was a pit at the bottom of which lay a hazel twig and a burnt bone from a human ear. Cremated bodies were found at various points on the surrounding circles, and there were both skeletons and cremations within the central chamber. There stands the pillar stone, blank, evocative, and rather frightening. Bryn is unique. It is also complex, and to do it justice one must buy the official guide (obtainable on the spot).

Although this is primarily a book about English prehistory, no description of chambered tombs would be complete without some reference to two of the greatest monuments of prehistoric times, the chambered tombs at New Grange in Ireland and Maes Howe in Scotland.

New Grange lies south of T26 (Drogheda-Slane), and is perhaps the greatest of all passage graves. Built about 2500 B.C. it consists today of a mound 40 feet high and 240 feet in diameter, surrounded by a circle of thirty-five stones and kerbed by 100 stones, many of which are decorated. A passage 60 feet long, 3 feet wide and of varying height, leads to a cruciform chamber 18 feet by 21 feet in plan and 19 feet 6 inches in height. This remarkable height was obtained by means of a cleverly-constructed corbel vault.

Apart from its size and comparative completeness, New Grange is worth visiting for the remarkable number of its decorated stones. Thirty are visible and there are many others which cannot be seen. Outside Ireland, there are only half-a-dozen examples of megalithic art in the whole of Great Britain. The decorations consist mainly of complex lozenges and spirals. The latter are probably stylized pictures of the eyes or breasts of the Earth Mother Goddess.

Similar rather less impressive mounds can be seen not far away at Dowth and Knowth.

These passage graves were built by people, originally traders and prospectors, who sailed in boats of skin, or perhaps of wood like those of Iberian fishermen today, whose craft still bear the Oculus, the eye of the goddess, on their prows, from the shores of Spain and Portugal to Brittany and Ireland. The indications are that they came from a society that already understood the working of metal and the settlements which they established in Ireland survived for 1,000 years into the Irish High Bronze Age about 1500 B.C.

In Scotland and Ireland, as in Wales, there is a cultural division. In south-west Scotland and north-east Ireland, there are chambered cairns of the Severn-Cotswold type. See, for instance, Carn Ban (NR/990262) at the southern end of the Isle of Arran.

From the New Grange area of Ireland the passage grave builders appear to have pushed north-east into Scotland, avoiding the areas which were already occupied and moving by way of the Hebrides and the Great Glen towards Caithness and the Orkneys. And it is precisely there in the Orkneys, at almost the extreme limit of the British Isles, that one finds Maes Howe (HY/318127) on the main island, one of the wonders of the prehistoric world.

A round mound 115 feet in diameter and 24 feet high covers a passage 36 feet long, constructed of slabs up to 18 feet in length, leads to a chamber 15 feet square and of sophisticated construction. Shelves are built into three of the walls, while the corners are strengthened by attached piers to support the corbelled vault that once rose to a height of 18 feet. This last was destroyed in 1861 and today Maes Howe is open to the sky, the corbelling now rising to a height of just under 13 feet.

Maes Howe has a secondary interest. Vikings on their way to the East broke in, probably during the winter of A.D. 1150–51. Two years later Earl Harold and his men sheltered there "while a snowstorm drove over them, and there two men of their band lost their wits, and that was a great hindrance to their journey". The runic inscriptions recording these visits are still there, together with the scratched outlines of a walrus, a serpent and a dragon.

To return to the exposed chambered tombs of southern Britain; many of them have lost their covering, leaving the stones of the burial chamber, often with a huge capstone, exposed to view. On some maps and in some descriptions, these are—not very scientifically—distinguished as dolmens or, in Wales, as cromlechau. Stark and dramatic against the sky, these are, for the ordinary observer 'prehistoric remains' *par excellence*, immediately recognizable, immediately romantic. One must remember that they were not intended to be seen. Time has exposed them—in one eighteenth-century engraving a patch of earth can still be seen covering part of the capstone, of what today is a completely free-standing, uncovered chamber.

The enclosed megalithic chamber and the exposed one evoke quite different emotions. To crawl down the passage or gallery within the first is to experience an indefinable, internal subconscious reaction. It is to come a little closer to the feelings of the remote ancestors who built the tomb. On the other hand, to see the huge stones of a tomb which has lost its covering is to experience a civilized, sophisticated reaction—more especially if one sees the stones dark against the evening sky or solidifying as one approaches through a mountain mist—which may be loosely defined as 'romantic'. Each type of reaction may be profound, but they differ absolutely in quality.

The romantic reaction led early enthusiasts to link the dolmen with the equally romantic druids (see pp. 144–8 below). In their eyes the huge capstone was obviously an altar and if it sloped a little—why, so much the better, that was clearly in order to let the blood run off. Thus in the eighteenth century a Chancellor of Bangor Cathedral could write enthusiastically:

"The Cromllech or Inclined Plane was notably well fitted for the Opening, Extension and Examination of the Entrails of any kind of victims; and its gradual Slope was very favourable to the descent of the flowing blood, as well as Other Liquids, a victim laid in such a position Could be better Observed by both the Priests and the People; and all the several Convulsive Agitations of the heart, Intestines, in the agonies of Death, be better seen, than either in an upright or a horizontal one."[1]

Pure fiction.

What were the real rites involved in the burial at a megalithic barrow? One cannot know; it is what Sir Thomas Browne would have called "a puzzling question" yet "not beyond all conjecture". An informed guess is permissible. It is at least likely to be nearer to the truth than the gory imaginings of Richard Farrington.

Professor Glyn Daniel refers to a description[2] of the probable burial rites carried out in Mycenean Greece, an area with which the megalithic tombs were distantly connected and from which

[1] Richard Farrington, *Snowdonia Druidica or the Druid Monuments of Snowdon* (MS in the National Library of Wales, Aberystwyth, dated 1769, pp. 42–3); quoted by Glyn Daniel, p. 47.
[2] Glyn Daniel, pp. 49–50, quoting Professor G. E. Mylonas writing in the *American Journal of Archaeology*, 1949, p. 56 *et seq.*

there were to be later cultural contacts with Wessex. These provide a possible parallel with the no doubt debased practices in use when burial took place in a British megalithic tomb.

The dead were left in a chamber tomb, the door was walled up, and a funeral feast was held. (The forecourt of a barrow could well have served for this purpose.) When a second death occurred, the tomb was re-opened, and the process was repeated until the bodies decomposed. Then space was made for the latest occupant by sweeping the earlier bones to one side. Once the body had disintegrated, the person it had represented no longer had need of anything.

If this, or something like it, occurred in Britain, it would explain many of the puzzling features of a megalithic tomb: the forecourt, the varied nature of the corpses, the fact that sometimes there seem to be far too many bones for the size of the chamber, the puzzling manner in which many of the bones have been tumbled together unceremoniously, like piles of sticks. Consider, for instance, the state of affairs at Lanhill (ST/877747) a Wiltshire barrow 3 miles out of Chippenham to the south of road A420 (Bristol-Chippenham). There in one small chamber measuring only 5 feet by 4 by 2 feet 5 inches there was found the remains of nine bodies ranging in age from one to 70 all piled at the back of the chamber while a single skeleton, that of the last-comer, held pride of place undisturbed in front of them.

In what language were these rites observed? Again, one cannot know, but clearly it would be speech unrelated to the Indo-European tongue from which almost all modern European languages are derived, since that was a later arrival. Possible descendants which have survived are Berber or Basque, and Professor Glyn Daniel is prepared to find in modern Basque fishermen a faint reflection of the Iberian megalithic seafarers. Catch your breath and listen when next you hear them round a café table in Guipuzcoa or Viscaya, for you may be hearing an echo from prehistory.

What brought the megalithic builders to these islands? Four rival theories hold the field and their supporters are usually prepared to defend their own pet explanation tooth and nail, but the uncommitted observer might be excused for supporting that the truth may lie in a combination of several—perhaps even of all—the suggested motives.

The distribution of tombs has been interpreted as indicating the movement of prospectors in search of the minerals—copper, tin and gold—that were essential to the Bronze Age economy which had already developed in southern Europe.

Others have read the tombs as evidence of the activities of what have been termed 'travelling undertakers', selling a method of securing immortality as elaborate as those patronized in twentieth-century California. This view shades imperceptibly into that which sees the tombs as the result of the missionary activity of the priests of the religion of the Earth Goddess.

Or perhaps the tombs are, more prosaically, only the remains left by men moved by ambition or necessity to carve out new territories for themselves?

Prospectors, undertakers, missionaries, colonists—whatever the drive, spiritual or economic, the new groups had come to stay, and eventually, in highland and lowland zones alike, there developed native hybrids—new communities, known as Secondary Neolithic.

IV

SECONDARY NEOLITHIC GROUPS:
2300 to 1800 B.C.

The previous chapter has already encroached on the period of time covered by this one. The centuries around the turn of the third millenium are ones in which exact chronological limits are impossible to observe. They are centuries during which cultural boundaries weaken and dissolve as communities interact one with another, producing hybrids. There is a new complexity which is not susceptible to the discipline of rigid patterns.

What happened was roughly as follows. The earlier Neolithic cultures were received by, responded to, and assimilated with, that of the already existing Mesolithic inhabitants. Native hunters from the earlier period and immigrant pastoralists from the later one intermingled in many areas and insular groups developed, communities peculiar to Britain. These are, in general, known as Secondary Neolithic. Archaeologists recognize two main types: the *Peterborough* and the *Rinyo-Clacton*.

The second of these lies largely outside the areas covered by this book. One cannot, though, omit all mention of it, for in one place the Rinyo-Clacton people have left an invaluable clue to the probable conditions of life in other areas.

They owe their rather cumbersome name to the fact that they are represented by remains found at Clacton in Essex and Rinyo in the Orkneys. There are virtually no intermediate links, yet a common way of life in these two widely-separated areas, improbable as that may seem, nevertheless appears almost certain.

It is the settlement at Skara Brae (HY/231187) in the Orkneys that is unique. Wood was rare—perhaps even non-existent—

and as a consequence the settlement was equipped with stone furniture, which has survived almost unchanged. From the remains at Skara Brae it is therefore possible to deduce what other groups, in areas in southern Britain, may have possessed in timber.

There are half-a-dozen huts, clustered together within a quarter of an acre. Dug into the sand, with dry-stone walls, the huts are about 15 feet square and are linked one with another by narrow passages. Originally these huts and passages were roofed with turf resting on driftwood and whalebones—the only supports available—and then covered with layer upon layer of rubbish. This almost mole-like existence was necessary in such an exposed place.

Within each hut there was a central hearth and beside it a clay oven, both fired by peat. Sunk into the floor were one or two stone-lined tanks filled with water, in which shell-fish—limpets and so on—were kept alive until they were required for eating. Stone-lined boxes were built on the floor against the walls to right and left of the door, where they were out of the draught, and were filled with heather and bracken to form beds. The right-hand bed was normally the larger. It is assumed that the master and his wife shared this while the rest of the family made do as best they could with the other one. Stone-slabbed cupboards and dressers were built into the other walls. (Looking at cottages on Achill Island, Eire, deserted after the Great Hunger of 1846, I saw precisely similar stone cupboards in the low walls on either side of the fire-place.)

The interior of the Skara Brae huts was dark and conditions, in spite of the sophistication of the fittings, were incredibly squalid. The floor is still, 3,000 years later, stained with sewage and, when first examined, was thick with the remains of ancient meals. Into the bedding there had fallen not only the understandable pins and beads, but also—a shoulder-blade shovel and a calf's head. Remote and isolated, the life of these northern Britons was not very far removed from that of their Mesolithic predecessors. If *they* had furniture, surely the more southern groups must have had something at least as good, now lost for ever?

The Peterborough culture, well-established in the south, owes its name to the area where it was first identified and not to its main settlements.

This was, one feels, in many ways a rather unattractive culture. It retained a strong admixture of Mesolithic characteristics. Its pottery, round-bottomed coiled pots ornamented with cord impressions or little marks made with a bone or twig, is heavy. Its members are found 'camping out' in the deserted ditches of Windmill Hill, or squatting among the bones of oxen, pigs, sheep and—the last turn of the screw—the remains of thousands upon thousands of slugs.

Nevertheless, this basic squalor gave the Peterborough communities a survival value. When, later, new invaders—Beaker and Bronze Age folk—eliminated or completely transformed the more settled, more civilized Neolithic groups, the Peterborough natives simply submerged to reappear in due course with their pottery—and therefore, it may be assumed, their way of living—unchanged. Asking little from life they found it correspondingly easy to survive in times of crisis. There is perhaps a lesson here for the twentieth century?

In Secondary Neolithic days, some of the Peterborough people, tough and knowledgeable about the pattern of the country, became suppliers of stone and flint axes—perhaps also of the red deer antlers used in mining—moving between the sources of supply in East Anglia, Cornwall and North Wales, and the areas of consumption in southern England.

They knew the trails, they were outside the more advanced Neolithic social systems, foot-loose middlemen, half poachers and half hawkers, they traded stone axes from the north and west to the comparatively wealthy farmers of Wessex. They were opening up trade routes that would, centuries later, bring metals south and so create the most brilliant of English prehistoric societies—the Wessex culture (see pp. 88–9).

The polished stone axe had become invaluable. Birch forest could be felled rapidly. One man could clear 600 square yards in a matter of twelve hours, but it involved a good deal of wear and tear on the axe-head, which would only last for about 100 trees. It was important to keep up the supply. The Peterborough traders probably camped at the quarries, living off the land in the traditional manner of their Mesolithic ancestors. There they roughed-out the axe-heads. Then they moved with their half-finished wares south, to areas where the main body of purchasers was to be found.

Take the Welsh trade as an example. Graig Lwyd at Penmaenmawr in Caernarvonshire was one factory. Another was at Mynydd Rhiw, Bryncoes, on the Llyn peninsula in Caernarvonshire. At Graig Lwyd the scree is thick with the spoil from the factory and with rejects—not only of axes, but also of chisels, hammers, adzes and so forth. A scatter of hearths exists and close by hazelnut shells, the evidence of the men who worked this quarry. From there the implements were moved south, either inland, or by water down the coast of Wales and then up the Severn estuary. In view of the weight involved it is likely that the bulk of the manufactures went by water. A Peterborough settlement has been found at Cefn Cilsanws on the south side of the Brecon Beacons, and there is evidence of a depot at Merthyr Mawr Warren, near Porthcawl, Glamorganshire, where the traders may have had a winter staging-post.

This highly-organized trade in a product vital to the existence of the more civilized south is one aspect of Secondary Neolithic civilization. Another is the creation in the south of new types of structure, the cursus and the henge monument. Collective burial in a chambered tomb was for a minority, but all might join in the construction of circles and of giant processional ways. Both are peculiar to Britain, both are impressive, both should be seen.

There is not much likelihood of anyone missing Stonehenge—which, in its earliest form, dates from this period—but the cursus, there and elsewhere, is less well-known.

The word *cursus* was the name given to a Roman race-course. It was first applied to English remains by the archaeologist, William Stukeley, in 1723. A British cursus is an earthen avenue, enclosed by a ditch and bank. In plan it does bear a faint resemblance to a Roman hippodrome, but the Romans had nothing to do with these enclosures, and it is quite uncertain whether or not they were used for races. They are best regarded as processional avenues, for use on politico-religious occasions, forerunners perhaps of the Bronze Age avenues of stones found on Dartmoor. A cursus is today, unfortunately, most impressive when seen from the air. At ground level it tends to be, if small, obliterated, while if it is large it is difficult to grasp it in totality.

These avenues were dug at some date between 3000 and 2000 B.C. but most probably towards the end of that period. They vary in length from a mere 200 yards to a giant 6 miles. They are often associated with, and sometimes aligned on, earthen long barrows and it is possible that the connection is closer than that, for the bank barrows are giants 600 feet and more in length from which the cursus may well have evolved (see p. 39).

Of these bank barrows, the greatest is at Maiden Castle (SY/668885) (see below, p. 154) where there is a mound a quarter of a mile long and 60 feet wide, which follows the ridge of the hill. This is classified as a 'long mound', an extension of the earthen long barrow, but it is likely that it also served as a ritual highway for processions. On its axis and near the eastern end there had been buried the dismembered body of a young man. It can be proved that the body was still covered with flesh when the dismemberment took place, and that first the head was cut off, then the legs and after them the arms. The pelvis had been split, and three attempts had been made to extract the brain from the skull, the last of which was successful. Sir Mortimer Wheeler is of the opinion "that the body had been cooked and eaten". This grisly ceremony was probably a foundation ritual.

Later activities have almost obliterated the mound at Maiden Castle. At Stonehenge to the north of A360 there are traces of a cursus, running east and west, 1¾ miles in length, 100 yards wide, enclosing an area of about 70 acres. It ends at a long barrow in the east and was probably built at the same time as the erection of Stonehenge I, the first temple on the site. Unfortunately, as at Maiden Castle, there is now little to see.

Undoubtedly the most dramatic cursus, the most rewarding to follow on the ground, is the one which runs parallel to road A354 (Blandford-Salisbury). Here there is an enclosure 6 miles in length. The width is about 100 yards, as at Stonehenge. At some stage the length of this cursus was doubled. The southern section, 3½ miles long, is the earlier. It start at Thickthorn Down (ST/971123), just west of a long barrow, and goes north-east. It is not easy to see until it reaches Gussage Hill (ST/996146) where it encloses a long barrow. The next 2 miles are the best. The cursus cuts across the Roman road known as Ackling Dyke—a bonus for the traveller —and the southern section finishes just short of the road to Cran-borne (B3081). The northern section is clear to begin with, but soon woods and ploughland make the going difficult. This section incorporates another long barrow and ends at two long barrows on Bokerley Down (SU/041188), just beyond the village of Pentridge.

The construction of this giant involved the moving of about 3,700,000 cubic feet of chalk as its builders cut directly across country, across valleys and ridges. The social imperative for an effort of this size must have been military or religious. A military purpose is out of the question. Clearly the cursus (and others like it) was a religious processional way.

Contemporary with these avenues are the earlier henge monu-ments, alternatively called ditched sanctuaries. The vagueness of these names reflects the uncertainty in the minds of archaeologists as to the exact function of these remains.

Anyone reading this book has presumably already a mental picture of Stonehenge. It is important to expunge this. The Stonehenge one sees today was not the Stonehenge built in Secondary Neolithic days, nor was the original structure in many ways a typical henge monument.

To begin with a definition: a henge monument is a circular enclosure, normally with an external ditch and an internal bank— a characteristic feature which helps the amateur to distinguish it from other forms of banked remains. The earlier (Secondary Neolithic) types have a single entrance, while those built at a later date by Beaker folk have two entrances opposite one another. They enclose various features. In general—they were a form of structure which lasted for 1,000 years, and naturally they changed in details —they surrounded some sort of wooden structure, while later ones were more likely to contain stones.

The variety of individual henge monuments is part of their charm. Their diameter may measure anything from 20 feet to 1,500 feet or more. They may be on high ground or on low-lying land. They may contain barrows or—posthumously so to say—a Norman church. At Avebury a village has used the bank and ditch as its walls. At Dorchester the Romans converted Maumbury Rings into an amphitheatre. Who can say for what purpose we use Stonehenge today?

Forty or fifty henge monuments and their relatives have been located so far, scattered from Cornwall to the Orkneys, and there are without doubt others waiting to be recognized, perhaps by the informed amateur.

The earliest large ones are probably the Sanctuary, Woodhenge and Stonehenge I, conveniently within 30 miles of one another by road.

The Sanctuary (SU/118679) lies just to the south of road A4 (Calne-Marlborough) 5 miles out of Marlborough. Finds are in the museum at Devizes. Today one sees rings of concrete pillars. A monument stood here for 4,000 years until the seventeenth century. Stukeley wrote: "It was a very few years ago, crown'd with a most beautiful temple of the Druids" and went on to describe how it was destroyed by a Farmer Griffin and how everyone sorrowed except "the person that gain'd the little dirty profit".

The development was complex, involving four phases of building and eight circles, and the traveller should consult the plan at the site. Basically, the first building was a simple wooden circle with a central post. This was later surrounded by a building, probably open to the sky at the centre, consisting of a roof carried on two circles of wooden posts. Later still a larger enclosure, also of wood, was put up. The sanctuary at this stage was similar to Woodhenge nearby, was the work of Secondary Neolithic people, and was probably in existence before there was anything at nearby Avebury. Later the Beaker people replaced the wooden building by two concentric circles of sarsen stones, and appear to have constructed the avenue that leads to Avebury.

Woodhenge (SU/150435) is about 2 miles north-east of Stonehenge, lying to the west of road A345 (Amesbury-Marlborough) about 1½ miles out of Amesbury. Here, too, the finds are in the museum at Devizes, and the circles on the site are marked by concrete posts.

Woodhenge consists of a slightly oval enclosure, with a maximum diameter of 220 feet. A bank, now obliterated by ploughing, lay outside a flat-bottomed ditch. There was one entrance to the north-east. Within are six circles of postholes, the largest—and these are very large indeed, 5 feet in diameter and 5 feet 8 inches deep—halfway to the centre. It is thought that these posts supported the ridge of a circular roof, which was pitched both inwards and outwards like a barn, its lower levels supported by lesser posts. The roof would be open to the sky.

Woodhenge is orientated to the midsummer sunrise. Just to the south of the centre there was found the skeleton of a 3 year old child, its skull split open, one of the few certain evidences of human sacrifice in Britain. Two votive axe-heads carved from chalk were also found.

Woodhenge has a special significance in archaeological history. Its existence was unsuspected until, in December 1926, Wing-Commander Insall, V.C., flying at a height of 2,000 feet, observed a pattern of rings on the ground. A new instrument had been added to the equipment of the prehistorian and the historian. Since that date tens of thousands of archaeological photographs have been taken and hundreds of unsuspected features have been observed for the first time. At least one university now has an official Curator in Aerial Photography, and all recognize the value of such work.

For the archaeologist, the aerial photograph has three main virtues. It can cover a comparatively large area and show the relationship between different remains in that area, making clear the whole length of the Dorset cursus or the distribution of barrows around Stonehenge, for instance, facts which are not immediately obvious on the ground.

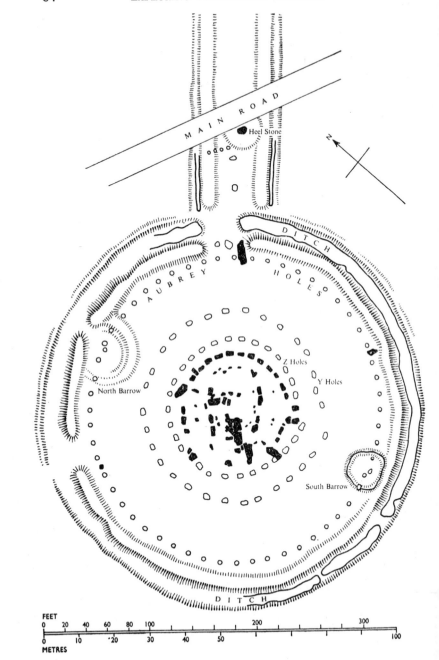

MAIN ROAD

Heel Stone

N

DITCH

AUBREY

HOLES

Z Holes

Y Holes

North Barrow

South Barrow

DITCH

FEET
0   20   40   60   80   100   200   300
0   10   20   30   40   50   100
METRES

Bryn Celli Ddu, chambered tomb. Entrance and carved stone.

The Neolithic settlement of Skara Brae. Stone 'furniture' can be seen in the nearest hut.

Silbury Hill. The quarry-ditch from which material for the hill was dug can be seen in the foreground.

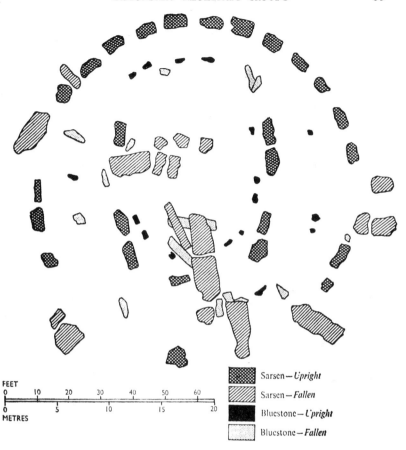

FEET

0   10   20   30   40   50   60

0   5   10   15   20
METRES

Sarsen — *Upright*

Sarsen — *Fallen*

Bluestone — *Upright*

Bluestone — *Fallen*

Stonehenge *(left)* Plan of the whole site. The stones are shown in black at the centre and enlarged in more detail *(above)* to show present situations and conditions.

(Reproduced by permission of the Central Office of Information)

Secondly, by taking photographs when the sun is low in the sky, the shadows cast by slight irregularities magnify these and reveal patterns inconspicuous to the earth-bound man. (Sometimes these features were in fact visible at ground level, but had just not been noticed. At Dowth, for example, in the Boyne area of Ireland, a circle was first discovered by aerial photography which is now quite clear to ground observers.)

E

Thirdly—and this is where Woodhenge literally comes into the picture—once the surface of the ground has been disturbed, the effect of that disturbance is for all practical purposes permanent. Holes filled or ditches raised consist of material which is never as compact as undisturbed subsoil and will always affect the density or colour of vegetation growing there.

The slight differences in height, colour or density of vegetation, indistinguishable at ground level, show up with dramatic clarity in an aerial photograph. These crop-markings are the X-rays of the archaeologist.

Stonehenge (SU/123422) lies in the angle between roads A303 (Wincanton-Amesbury) and A344 (Shrewton-Amesbury) about 2 miles out of Amesbury.

As it now stands it consists of no fewer than five successive constructions, built by differing peoples using various materials and having perhaps different ends in view. Stonehenge I was the creation of Secondary Neolithic people, probably about 2200 B.C. Most of this first structure can still be seen—bank and ditch, Heel Stone and Aubrey Holes. It consisted of an outer bank 380 feet in diameter, within that a ditch, and within this a second bank of chalk, 320 feet in diameter, 20 feet wide and 6 feet high. A single causeway about 35 feet wide led into this ditched sanctuary from the north-east. Close to the entrance and outside it this causeway incorporates a possibly earlier huge sarsen block weighing about 35 tons and now called the Heel Stone. (As in the case of other named stones, the name has no archaeological significance. On the outer face the eye of faith can see a large heelprint. The Devil threw the stone at a Friar, hitting him on the heel.) There is a ditch round this stone.

Where the causeway entered the sanctuary there was probably some sort of entrance gateway. Within the inner bank the builders made a circle of 56 holes, 16 feet apart. These are now known as the Aubrey Holes, after John Aubrey (1626–97) who first commented on them. About half of these holes are now marked by white chalk circles. Their average depth is about 2 feet 6 inches and many of them have been found to contain cremations. A radio carbon dating of the material indicated a date between 2123 and 1573 B.C. For other reasons, the earlier date is the more probable.

Stonehenge I, as described, remained for 500 years until, about 1700 B.C., the Beaker folk remodelled it, building what archaeologists know as Stonehenge II, which is described on pages 80–1.

Stonehenge is the king of henge monuments, but many others

are worth a visit. There is, for instance, Marden (SU/091584), 1,200 feet in diameter—turn north off road A342 5 miles east of Devizes—a giant largely uninvestigated and, at least as far as the ordinary traveller is concerned, unvisited.

Two small henge monuments of especial interest by reason of their eccentric history are Maumbury Rings and Knowlton in Dorset.

Maumbury Rings (SY/690899) is in Dorchester in the south of the town to the east of road A354 (Weymouth). The Rings is 350 feet in diameter, with a bank 15 feet high and, as usual, an inside ditch. Finds are in the Dorchester Museum. The interest here lies in the uses to which the enclosure was later put. The Romans converted it into an amphitheatre, for which purpose it was admirably suited, and the results of this conversion are clear today. Fifteen hundred years later, in 1642, the site was used again, this time for Royalist gun emplacements during the Civil War. In 1705 a woman who had killed her husband was burnt to death there before, it is said, 10,000 spectators. In 1723 Stukeley, visiting the Rings, found the interior under the plough. Indignant, he wrote "never did I see corn growing, which of itself is an agreeable sight, with so much indignation as in this noble concavity. . . ."

Knowlton Circles (SU/024100–025102) are three henge monuments, built along a north-west/south-east axis, 3 miles south of Cranborne on B3078 (Wimborne Minster), the road cutting the southernmost circle, 800 feet in diameter.

It is, though, the central circle at which one must look. This is, for my money, one of the most romantic sites in England. The bank and ditch (350 feet in diameter) are well-preserved, with enough trees growing on them to give the scene perspective and beauty, but not so many that the plan of the structure is concealed. Then, within the circle, there are the ruins of a twelfth-to-sixteenth-century church, hung with ivy and partly overgrown. Seen in almost any light and from almost any angle, the grouping of bank, trees and church is highly picturesque, in the best sense.

The site also has a sociological fascination, with the Christian church deliberately placed at the centre of the heathen shrine. Were pagan ceremonies still being celebrated here 3,000 years after the circle was dug, ceremonies that required this exorcism? Whatever the explanation, to visit Knowlton is a powerful experience.

At Gorsey Bigbury (ST/484558) one is down to earth again, as befits perhaps the bare Mendips. To reach the site, leave road A38 (Bridgwater-Bristol) about one mile south of Churchill for Shipham. Pass through that village and take the first turning left for Charterhouse. Gorsey Bigbury is south of the road, one mile short of Charterhouse, on the land of Lower Farm, from which permission to visit it should be obtained. Here the bank is about 200 feet in diameter and the ditch was cut in places into the living rock. There is one entrance, facing north. After the sanctuary was completed, it was probably abandoned. Remains in the south-east part of the ditch show that the next invaders, Beaker people, lived there, cooking and eating their food. It looks as though Gorsey Bigbury may have been occupied by these new men almost as soon as it was finished.

Continue through Charterhouse to the minor road junction with B3135 from Cheddar, turn left along this road and after a little more than a mile the southernmost of Priddy Circles (ST/540527) lies on your left-hand. These are perhaps not worth a special visit, but they can be combined with Gorsey Bigbury conveniently. Not a great deal is yet known about these four embankments: they have single entrances (which is typical) and a ditch outside the bank (which is not). There are indications that the bank of the southern circle was piled up between a double row of wooden posts. They are probably later (1600 B.C. to 1350 B.C.) than Beaker times.

The main henge monuments all lies in the Wessex area. There are a few examples in the south-west, the one where there is probably most to see being at Castilly (SX/031627), 4 miles out of Bodmin and just south of road A30 (St. Austell-Bodmin). Here the bank is oval (161 feet by 97 feet) with a single opening to the north-west. Outside the South-west of England, the most rewarding examples are in the northern counties. Later in date, though they probably derive at least in part from the southern group, they are described in the next chapter (see p. 83).

One monument of Secondary Neolithic date is, in the strict sense, unique.

Halfway between Calne and Marlborough, on the north side of road A4, and almost opposite the West Kennet long barrow, stands the immense green artificial mound of Silbury Hill (SW/100685). Many natural mounds look artificial, Silbury is so huge that it looks natural. Yet it is man-made—the largest structure of its kind in Europe. It covers $5\frac{1}{4}$ acres and originally contained about 14 million cubic feet, $6\frac{1}{2}$ million cubic feet of

man-moved earth resting on a base of natural chalk. It was surrounded by a ditch 25 feet wide and about 16 feet deep from which
the material for the hill was taken.

Like Stonehenge, legend surrounds Silbury. Aubrey in the
seventeenth century recorded that the tradition was that a king
"was buried here on horseback and that the hill was raised while
a posset of milk was seething".

Six times men have tried to discover the secret of the Hill. In
1776 the Duke of Northumberland brought tin-miners from Cornwall and sank a shaft from top to bottom. Result—nothing but
a small piece of oak. Over seventy years later in 1849 the Dean
of Hereford supervised the construction of a tunnel from circumference to centre. Result—nothing but the information that at
the centre there was a smaller, primary mound built up of layers
of chalk, clay and turf, and fragments of 'a sort of string' of
twisted grass. In 1867 excavation on the east side revealed that
the Roman Road did not pass beneath the mound; indeed, it
swerved to avoid Silbury, thus proving that the mound was at
least pre-Roman. In 1886 pits dug in the ditch showed that it was
largely filled with weathered chalk from the Hill, which must have
been originally a third larger than it is today. In 1922 Sir Flinders
Petrie failed to find an entrance, but discovered that the mound
had been raised in horizontal layers and not tipped to form a
cone.

A little had been found out concerning the construction of
Silbury, but of material remains, of clues to the real purpose of
this immense product of social activity—nothing.

In the sixties the B.B.C. decided to organize and finance a series
of operations conducted over a number of years, that would, at
last, crack the secret of Silbury Hill and in 1968 a new tunnel was
excavated close to that of 1849.

It showed that the erection comprised three stages. First a
mound 120 feet in diameter and 18 feet high was raised consisting
of a gravel core, faced with turf and surrounded by a circle of
wooden sticks. This core was covered by four layers, each 2 feet
thick, of different mineral materials—chalk, gravel, clay. Next, this
core was covered with a mound of chalk with a base 240 feet in
diameter and probably about 55 feet in height. Before this was
finished, yet another enlargement took place, producing the present
Hill, over 550 feet in diameter and over 130 feet in height.

More information about the method of construction had been
obtained—of artificial remains, still nothing.

Of material non-man-made remains, though, a fascinating variety. The central core of stacked turf contained, unaffected by the centuries, the grass and mosses, the insects and the snails, the twigs and the beetles, that had lived in the age when Silbury was raised. Professor Atkinson has spoken of "a biological sandwich, en ecological cold-store", a shuttered window which has opened to reveal a whole prehistoric landscape, hitherto unknown. Radio carbon datings have pushed back the probable date of construction into Secondary Neolithic times, but the purpose of the hill remains as mysterious as ever.

V

THE BEAKER PEOPLE:

2000 to 1600 B.C.

The peasant life of the Secondary Neolithic communities was—at least in the south of Britain—abruptly changed by the arrival of fresh immigrants.

In western Europe new groups had been evolving: copper workers in Spain and Portugal; archer pastoralists around the Baltic; battle-axe people in the Rhineland. The archer pastoralists herded sheep and used arrows with barbed flint heads. Their graves often contained small stone plaques designed to be strapped on the left wrist to protect it from the flick of the bowstring. The battle-axe people owe their dramatic name to their use of stone replicas of the rare and expensive bronze axe. The heads are of perforated stone, on the average about 9 inches in length, of great intrinsic beauty. It is clear that the owner prized the external appearance of an axe-head of red Cornish tourmaline or flecked Prescelly blue for reasons—aesthetic, religious, or perhaps merely social—that were not based on mere utility.

The groups flowed and fused and hybridized long before their descendants had reached the British Isles, and elements from all these northern and western cultures entered Britain—a little bronze, still very rare; the renewed use of the bow; the pierced stone axe-heads. The main invaders came as small warrior-bands, perhaps not more than a few hundred in numbers, practising inhumation instead of cremation, growing barley instead of wheat, and making the distinctive form of pot from which they have acquired their name.

The earliest arrivals reached Britain from Spain by way of

Brittany along the western sea route. They seem to have penetrated the interior by way of the Christchurch area and perhaps
also the Thames valley. Other groups came slightly later from
north-east Europe by the eastern route, settling on the low-lying
coast from Kent to Aberdeen, with a strong concentration on that
part between the Wash and Flamborough Head.

These Beaker folk straddle the period that includes the end of
the New Stone Age and the opening of the Bronze Age. In prehistory especially it is unreal to assume that the various 'ages' were
distinct, following on one from another in the way that the reigns
of kings succeed one another in historical times. On the contrary
there is always an overlap of centuries as one group of techniques
supersedes, gradually and patchily, another.

The Beaker warrior bands and their chieftains brought new ideas
and new racial types to Britain. They knew about metal and perhaps carried some with them, but they were primarily a stone-
using people. In this country their age is very much one of tran-
sition. It is, too, one of even greater variation than formerly
between one area and another as these continued to develop at
different speeds and to contain different racial mixtures.

They were powerful people, short, heavy-boned and muscular,
their skulls of the round headed (brachycephalic) type, a sharp contrast with the small long-headed Neolithic inhabitants. The Beakers
from which they get their name are rather well-made pots, standing about 8 inches high, with a clearly defined neck and a flared
mouth. They developed many variations but there is no mistaking
the characteristic profile. It is the easiest of all for the non-
specialist to recognize.

The clay was fired at a high temperature using a forced draught
—a technique significantly similar to that needed for metal-smelt-
ing. The relatively thin ware that resulted is usually a brightish
red or buff and is ornamented with panels or bands of decoration
made by the impression of a cord, or with notches produced by the
use of a square-toothed comb.

These beakers probably contained a sort of beer made from fer-
mented barley and one of them is normally found in a Beaker
burial, either at the head or the feet of the crouched skeleton. It
would appear that the Beaker chieftains were buried with the
equivalent of a pint of bitter close at hand.

The pots come from the graves, and burials are the main,
indeed almost the only source of information, knowledge of
Beaker life being limited and determined by the survival of a

fairly wide range of goods from Beaker death. Of anything that was not or could not be buried we know almost nothing.

This reliance on the type of objects that may have survived is one of the permanent limitations on the prehistorian's knowledge. The picture of different cultures acquires a distinctive and perhaps quite inaccurate tone from the accidents of survival. In general, for instance, what is known of the Beaker folk comes from their tombs; what is known of the much later Iron Age does not come from their tombs, but from their settlements.

With reference to this general point, Sir Mortimer Wheeler has commented on the nice significance of some words in Sermon XV of John Donne:

> The ashes of an Oak in the Chimney are no epitaph of that Oak, to tell me how high or how large that was; it tells me not what flocks it sheltered while it stood, nor what men it hurt when it fell. The dust of great persons' graves is speechless, too; it says nothing, it distinguishes nothing. As soon the dust of a wretch whom thou wouldst not, as of a prince whom thou couldst not look upon will trouble thine eyes if the wind blow it thither; and when a whirle-wind hath blown the dust of the Churchyard into the Church, and the man sweeps out the dust of the Church into the Churchyard, who will undertake to sift these dusts, and to pronounce, this is the Patrician, this is the noble flour, and this the yeoman, this the Plebeian bran?

We do not know what clothes the Beaker folk wore, but we do know that they made cloth from wool and a sort of linen from flax or from nettle-fibre—the latter a material still in use in Scandinavia in the nineteenth century—for tatters of these materials have been recovered from their graves. Buckles, too, have been found, together with conical buttons or toggles of shale, jet and bone. Buttons and trousers, those symbols of twentieth-century man, were probably the invention of North European groups. The warmer South of Europe tended to wear a tunic and cloak, held in place by a belt and large brooches.

Beaker folk seem to have been largely nomadic, though the important part played by barley in their lives implies a certain degree of stability. Wheat had been the predominant crop in Neolithic days, now 85 per cent of the crop was barley and wheat did not again reach 20 per cent of the total crop for 1,000 years.

There is hardly any evidence for the form of their settlements. They camped out in the ditches of earlier cultures (as at Gorsey

Bigbury), and rare traces of shallow pits and wattle-hurdling have been found, as primitive as those of long ago Mesolithic man. It was at about this time that the climate became warmer and drier (Sub-Boreal), a fact which may help to account for the flimsiness of these shelters.

The enduring remains are their temples and their graves. For the former they often took over, or imitated, existing monuments like Stonehenge I, adapting them to their own requirements and transforming them into stone structures. In place of the Neolithic communal cremation the Beaker people introduced the practice of individual burial.

The first Beaker graves are small circular affairs, often not more than a couple of feet in height, in which the body lies on its side, contracted, with its knees drawn up towards its ribs, as in the womb. Soon these rather unspectacular interments were in many areas superseded or supplemented by one of the most important, widespread and easily recognizable forms of prehistoric construction, the round barrow. The new shape survived in various forms throughout the Bronze Age—and indeed, intermittently, into Saxon times over 2,000 years later.

A round barrow is, in its simplest form, a circular earth mound looking today rather like a green plum pudding, often surrounded by a ditch from which the material that composed it was dug. This type, known as a bowl barrow, makes up the vast majority of all round barrows. In Wessex, where round barrows are thicker on the ground than anywhere else, out of about 6,000 round barrows still visible, perhaps 5,500 are of this basic bowl shape. Of these about 1,000 date from the Beaker period. It is best, however to consider these Wessex barrows in the period of the round barrow's heyday, the Bronze Age (see pp. 102–7).

On the east coast, where the Beaker people arrived rather later than in the south, there is interesting evidence of a compromise between existing customs and those of the newcomers.

In this connection the barrow at Duggleby Howe (SE/881669) is worth a visit. Leave road A64 (York-Scarborough) at Norton, taking B1248 and, where this road forks, following B1253 to Duggleby. The Howe lies on the east side of this road, a little beyond the village. Finds in the Transport Museum at Hull.

It is one of the largest round barrows, apparently a compromise between the large Neolithic long barrow and the usually much smaller round barrow, being 120 feet in diameter and originally about 30 feet high. Within there was an Irish stew of burial practices: single inhumations; inhumation in groups; cremations. These last consisted of remains collected from pyres somewhere else. A number of bone skewers about 9 inches long were found; these are thought to have fastened the bags in which the ashes were contained, though the bags themselves have decayed. The whole collection indicates a mixture of rites, of cultures, of peoples. It lies within the period 2100 to 1700 B.C.

Similar conclusions can be drawn from other burials in Yorkshire where a round barrow (Beaker practice) covers cremated burials (Neolithic practice).

An interesting Beaker burial was excavated in 1851 by Lord Londesborough, at Kelleythorpe, near Driffield in the East Riding. Inside a round barrow, the skeleton of a Beaker man was found in a stone box, lying in the crouched position on his left side. On his right arm there had been a perforated stone wrist guard with gold studs of the sort used by archers. Behind him was a wooden-handled copper knife. At his neck were three amber buttons and scraps of the linen clothes had survived beneath the bones. Behind his legs was placed the statutory beaker and—most evocative of all—in the space between his elbows and his knees there lay the head of a hawk. The objects suggest the grave of a hunting chieftain of fame and power.

In Yorkshire, too, there are from the Beaker period the Windypits burials. The Windypits are natural fissures in the limestone in the neighbourhood of the river Rye, north-west of Hawnby. In one of these, Antofts, at a depth of 80 feet, there were found the remains of eight persons and a number of beakers. There were also signs that a fire had been lit and used to cook an ox, the split bones of which together with those of pig, sheep and badger, lay round about. Radio carbon methods give a date of about 1800 B.C.

The other enduring remains of Beaker men are their temples. Though few in number, the Beaker folk clearly exercised a strong control, either by force or through influence, over the local people. Otherwise the construction of large embanked enclosures and stone circles would clearly have been impossible. Their influence may have rested partly on the possession of at least a few artefacts of copper and gold. One of their main activities was connected with their position as a link in the trade routes in these raw materials between the sources of supply in Ireland and the English lowlands—routes that had already been opened up by the earlier trade in stone axes.

In the south the Beaker people were almost certainly responsible for the inner circle at Avebury, the avenue near it, and the later reconstruction of Avebury. They built the double circles at the sanctuary, the monuments at Stanton Drew, and the embankment of Durrington Walls (SU/150437), a monster circle 1,600 feet in diameter, its bank and ditch 100 feet wide, lying across road A345 (Amesbury-Pewsey). Finds from Durrington are in Salisbury Museum. Most important of all, they reconstructed Stonehenge.

Avebury (SU/103700), 17 miles to the north of Stonehenge, is, like its better-known neighbour, one of the key centres in British —indeed, in European—prehistory. It lies on road A361, halfway between Swindon and Devizes, only a mile or two away from Windmill Hill. Finds are in Avebury Museum. It is one of the few sites which it is impossible to fail to discover, for the main road runs through the middle of this unique monument.

Nevertheless, in spite of its position and although it is very much larger than Stonehenge, Avebury was apparently not described in any detail until the mid-seventeenth century, when the Wiltshire antiquary John Aubrey wrote enthusiastically of what he saw, declaring that Avebury surpassed Stonehenge "as a cathedral doth a parish church".

Pepys, with his flair for recording what was curious and significant, visited Avebury not long after Aubrey: "rode all day with some trouble for fear of being put out of our way over the Downes, where the life of the shepherds is, in fair weather only, pretty. In the afternoon came to Avebury, where, seeing great stones like those of Stonage [Stonehenge] standing up, I stopped and took a countryman of that town, and he carried me and shewed me a place trenched in like Old Sarum almost, with great stones pitched in it, some bigger than those at Stonage in figure, to my great admiration: and he told me that most people of learning coming by do come and view them, and that the King [Charles II] did so: and that the Mount cast hard by is called Selbury [Silbury], from one King Seall buried there, as tradition says."

Avebury consists of a huge circular earthwork, within which is the Great Circle and two smaller circles. The earthen bank, originally white but now grass-grown, is 20 feet high, 75 feet wide at its base. Within this there is a flat platform about 15 feet wide and then the ditch from which the material for the bank was taken. The ditch was flat-bottomed, 30 feet deep, 15 feet wide at its base and 40 feet wide at ground level. Today this colossal

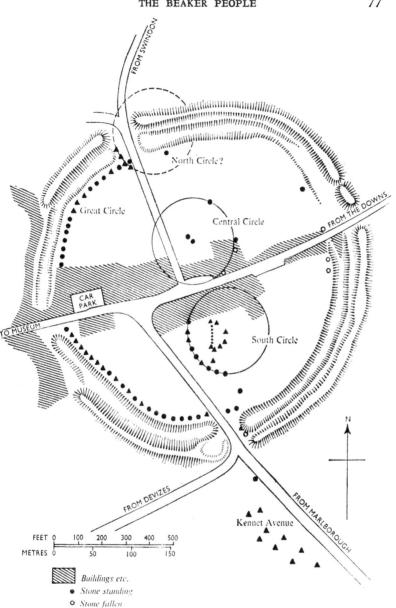

Plan of the Avebury Circles and Kennet Avenue
(Reproduced by permission of the Central Office of Information)

trench is half-filled with the soil of millenia, yet its size is still impressive. The outer bank, 1,400 feet in diameter, encloses 28 acres. There were four entrances set 90 degrees apart. These are now occupied by the four roads which meet in the village itself.

Within the ditch stands the remains of the Great Circle of about 100 sarsen stones—huge affairs, the largest, near the entrances, weighing over 40 tons. They have not been squared up as at Stonehenge and are, I think, more dramatic in their jagged crudity. There appear to be two main shapes, a vertical pillar and a lozenge, which may represent the male and female principles. Most of the stones still standing today are in the north-western quadrant. From the Devizes road, when you reach the ditch, turn left for this section.

Inside the Great Circle there are two smaller circles, the Central Circle and the South Circle. The Central Circle—the Swindon road intersects it—was 320 feet in diameter and made up of thirty stones. Only four of these are still standing, two on the circumference, two at the centre where there were once three arranged in a D-shaped pattern known as the Cove. (For similar structures, see Stanton Drew, p. 79, and Arbor Law, p. 83.) The South Circle was rather larger and was made up of thirty-two stones. Five stones are still in place and the sites of another four are marked by concrete blocks. West of its centre there was apparently a D-shaped arrangement of small stones.

Avebury has suffered more than Stonehenge at the hands of later generations, especially in the eighteenth century. Stonehenge has been to some extent protected until recently by its isolation, but Avebury contained an entire community. In the circumstances perhaps we should be grateful that anything at all has survived, for it is clear that it is only the huge scale of Avebury that has protected it from complete destruction.

The first full description of Avebury was that of William Stukeley in his *Abury* (1743), a valuable and infuriating account for it describes what has since disappeared and the methods by which the change was effected.

In 1722 Stukeley counted seventy-two stones; thirty years ago there were only nineteen still standing. Some were used for building; Stukeley says that a stone from the South Circle was used to build the dining-room end of the 'Red Lion'. Most were broken up. He recounts how, in order to clear the ground, farmers heated the stones until they were brittle, smashed them, and levelled the ground: "The method is to dig a pit by the side of the stone, till it falls down, then to burn many loads of straw under it. They draw lines along it when heated, and then with smart strokes of a great sledge-hammer, its prodigious bulk is divided into lesser parts." Stukeley felt a compassion for the stones as though they had been human beings burnt at the stake. He drew a picture of the destruction of one with the title *An Abury Atto da fe. May 20 1724.* For him Avebury was ". . . the most august work at this day upon the face of the earth" and its construction showed "a notorious grandeur of taste, a justness of plan, an apparent symmetry and a sufficient niceness in the execution: in compass very extensive, in effect magnificent and agreeable. The boldness of the imagination we cannot sufficiently admire."

Not all the destruction was in the eighteenth century. On at least one earlier occasion Avebury hit back. Early in the fourteenth century a man, a barber-surgeon, was caught and killed when the stone he was helping to remove fell and crushed him. His remains have been discovered and can be seen in the museum at Avebury. There are coins of Edward I's day, a lancet and a pair of scissors—the earliest known example in England.

Connected with Avebury are the Avenue and Sanctuary (for the latter, see pp. 62–3). Kennet Avenue runs south-east from Avebury (on the right of the minor road to Marlborough). Forty-nine feet wide, it consists of pairs of sarsens 80 feet apart and from Avebury for nearly a mile and a half. Some of the stones can be seen and the position of many more is marked by concrete blocks. Stukeley wrote that in the seventeenth century "the Kennet Avenue was entire, from end to end". The avenue does not connect comfortably with the great circle and there are various minor details—not observable by the traveller—which suggest that the final Avebury complex is the result of two phases of building. Phase I consisted of the Central and Southern Circles and the Avenue; Phase II was marked by the construction of the outer bank, ditch and Great Circle, and a realignment of the end of the Avenue.

At Avebury one sees how stone circles and embanked enclosures shade imperceptibly into one another. They are notoriously difficult to date, or even to place definitely within a cultural context. It seems probable, though that Stanton Drew (ST/603630) dates from the same period as Avebury. Take road A37 from Bristol in the direction of Wells; after 4 or five miles fork right along B3130 and then after another mile or so left to the village of Stanton Drew.

The Stanton Drew group consists of three circles, two avenues, a cove and an isolated stone. In the village, behind the Druid's Arms, stands the cove, a *D*-shaped setting of three stones, one of which has fallen. The south-west circle has twelve stones and a diameter of rather over 140 feet. It stands south of Stanton Drew church, in an orchard. A direct line from the cove to the north-east leads one to the central and north-eastern circles. The central circle is the larger, about 360 feet in diameter and now consisting of twenty-seven stones. A short avenue leads on towards the River Chew. The north-eastern circle has a diameter of just under 100 feet and is composed of eight stones—there were probably never any more—and an avenue joining that from the centre circle. A line projected from the south-west circle through the central circle and on for about a quarter of a mile will strike an isolated stone, known as Hauteville's Quoit. (The Hautevilles lived in the thirteenth century, 3,000 years later!) Originally there were two stones here.

The avenues support the view that this whole group of monuments was constructed by the Beaker people. The majority of the stones are of a local conglomerate and are undressed. Their rough, red, lumpy appearance gives them great authority.

At Stonehenge the Beaker people set to work to alter Stonehenge I (see p. 66), probably in about 1700 B.C. The result was a structure, Stonehenge II, of which so little now remains that its existence was not clearly recognized until 1954.

The construction of Stonehenge II involved the moving of about eighty bluestones, each weighing 4 tons, from the Prescelly Mountains in Pembrokeshire to Stonehenge, the most likely route involving a journey of 240 miles. How this astounding operation was carried out is described on p. 98). The bluestones are blocks of spotted dolerite, stones flecked with white and pink felspar. The area from which they came was an important producer of ground stone axes.

Once safely at Stonehenge, the bluestones were erected in a double circle with diameters of 88 feet and 76 feet within the existing enclosures. Their position is shown on plans of Stonehenge as occupying the Q and R holes. The entrance to this circle was on the north-east and was exactly aligned on the point where the sun would rise on the longest day of the year. This involved widening the gap in the old embankment, which was a little north of the required setting. Beyond this opening an avenue of earth 47 feet wide was constructed, swinging in a rough semi-circle to the River Avon at West Amesbury. It is thought that it marks the route by which the bluestones were hauled up from the Avon to Stonehenge. Very little of it can be seen at ground level today except close to Stonehenge itself, on the north side of road A344 to Shrewton.

It is very probable that Stonehenge II was never completed. There is a gap in the western arc of the circle, and two pits for entrance stones were dug but certainly never used. The reason is not difficult to guess. By 1600 B.C. the brilliant Wessex culture had developed and Stonehenge was being rebuilt in a much grander way (Stonehenge IIIa, see pp. 89–90).

The stone circle came, during the second millenium, to dominate the scene. In certain places the standing stone and the stone avenue accompanied it. In the less highly developed areas these monuments were being put up at time when Wessex had already entered the Bronze Age. Cultures flower and decay, overlapping in time as they do so. It seems logical to consider here the more interesting circles in other parts of the country, while noting that archaeological works tend to describe them under the blanket heading Neolithic and Bronze Age, thus indicating the existence of a wide spectrum of uncertainty.

Cornwall, well within the Megalithic culture-area, contains seven free-standing stone circles, most of them rather small. Indeed, it must be emphasized that, after Stonehenge, Avebury and Stanton Drew, almost any circle will come as something of an anti-climax. Nevertheless, the smaller circles have their virtues. For one thing, they are usually remote. One has them to oneself, and their setting often enhances their attraction. For another, consider their names—and the legends that gave them those names; it is hard to resist visiting sites with such names as The Grey Wethers, The Nine Maidens, The Carles or The Whispering Knights.

From the Cornish group one might select Boscawen-Un (SW/413274) between Penzance and Land's End, a quarter of a mile south of A30 a circle about 75 feet across, with a larger stone at the centre. Another is the Hurlers (SX/258714), 'men sometime transformed into stones, for profaning the Lord's Day, with hurling the ball', between Liskeard and Launceston, on B3254 1½ miles west of Upton Cross, three circles each over 100 feet across and each originally of about thirty stones; here an interesting point is that the northern one seems originally to have been paved and connected with the centre one by granite *pavé* 6 feet

F

wide. There is also the Merry Maidens (SW/432245) 1½ miles south-east of St. Buryan. This last is a good circle, 80 feet across with nineteen stones and with two very large stones, the Pipers, a quarter of a mile to the north-east. Here the legend is that girls were dancing, on the Sabbath, to the pipers' music, and all were suitably punished. The Stripple Stones (SX/144752), perhaps a little earlier than the others, for it consists of an earthen bank and ditch containing a ring of fifteen stones and a central emblem, lies on Bodmin Moor one mile north-west of road A30, 7 miles out of Bodmin on the way to Launceston.

In Devon there are on Dartmoor eleven stone circles, most of them rather small. The moor is in every way unique, and needs a book to itself. A useful cheap guide, which covers everything, not merely archaeology, is the H.M.S.O. publication *Dartmoor*.

The most interesting circles are those of the Grey Wethers (SX/638832). Leave B3212 (Moretonhampstead-Yelverton) at Postbridge. The two circles lie 3 miles to the north on the watershed between the Teign and the East Dart. Keep an eye on the mist. An easier circle to reach is that of Scorhill (SX/655874). Follow the lane from Gidleigh west past Berrydown for a little less than 2 miles.

There are three stone circles on Exmoor, none of them very impressive. The best is a rather late example at Withypool (SS/836343) half a mile to the south of the minor road that leads from Withypool to—eventually—South Molton.

In the Wessex area the great circles have already been described. A lesser example to the south is that of the Nine Stones (SY/611904) in Dorset. It lies on the south side of road A35 (Exeter-Dorchester), half a mile west of Winterbourne Abbas. Nine stones stand out of an original ten. The iron railings are probably necessary but do not improve the site.

North of Wessex a fine group is that of the King's Men or Whispering Knights (Rollright Stones, SP/296308) just west of road A34 (Oxford-Stratford) and half a mile north of the village of Little Rollright. They make up a circle of stones—it is said that their number cannot be counted—100 feet across, and the tomb referred to on p. 49. Here a certain king was advancing, presumably from the west, when he met a witch, who promised him that after advancing seven more paces

If Long Compton thou canst see,
King of England thou shalt be.

Long Compton was the next village, lying just over the crest of the hill. The king walked forward—and found his view blocked by a long earthen mound. The witch commented

> As Long Compton thou canst not see
> King of England thou shalt not be.
> Rise up, stick, and stand still stone,
> For King of England thou shalt be none;
> Thou and thy men hoar stones shall be
> And I myself an elder tree.

In Wales there are a number of small stone circles of the type already noticed in Cornwall and on Dartmoor. For the traveller the situation is complicated, both here and in the South-west, by the fact that what appear to be stone circles are in some places the kerbstones of barrows and in others the stone footing of huts. Any identification on the spot requires accurate knowledge or a detailed guide.

In North Wales, the Druids' Circle is on Penmaenmawr (SH/723747), off the road from Penmaenmawr itself to Bryn Dervydd. Although damaged by quarrying, the eastern part is intact. A circle of tall stones stand within a circular bank, with a core of small stones, about 8 feet wide. The central area was originally paved with white quartz. A child about 11 years old was buried at the centre. The entrance, now destroyed, was from the west. There is a good reason for visiting this circle, since it can easily be combined with the site of the Neolithic axe factory (SH/720760) (see p. 34) just to the west.

The most interesting circle in South Wales is one that has also suffered at the hand of later generations, but in a different way. It lies by road A4120 out of Aberystwyth in the village of Ysbyty Cynfyn (SN/752791). Here a Christian church was built inside the bank, which is now largely crowned by the church wall. Stones from the circle can be recognized in the wall and acting as gateposts, while a single stone stands to the north in its original position. Here, as at Knowlton and perhaps Avebury, there has been an attempt by a later religion to take over the sanctity or to exorcise the influence of an earlier form of worship.

Returning to England, and moving north, one should see Arbor Low (SK/160636), standing near Parsley Hay one mile to the east of road A515 (Buxton-Ashbourne). A bank 250 feet in diameter and 7 feet high surrounds a ditch 30 feet wide which in turn surrounds a stone circle 150 feet in diameter with a central cove. All the stones are now lying on the ground and as no pits have been found it is thought possible that the stones may only have been wedged upright, which would account for their collapsed state today.

Even so Arbor Low remains a curiously impressive site. There are two entrances, north and south. Just to the east of the south entrance there is a round barrow built into the side of the embankment. Some of the finds from Arbor Low are in the museum at Buxton 8 miles to the north.

North again, in Yorkshire, one should see the Thornborough Circles (SE/285795). These are henge monuments—i.e. embankments not stone circles—but probably of the Beaker period. The three circles lie north-east of West Tanfield, itself on road A6108 (Ripon-Leyburn) about 6 miles north of Ripon.

Each of the circles is about 800 feet in diameter and consists of a bank 10 feet high, with a ditch both inside and—unusually— outside it. There are two entrances, north-west and south-east. An interesting discovery is that the banks had apparently been coated with white crystals of gypsum, found locally, presumably to imitate the brilliant white chalk embankments in southern England. The central circle is the easiest to reach, the northern one is the best preserved, but it is heavily wooded.

There are other circles, less impressive, but presumably part of the same religious grouping—the largest in the north—at Cana (SE/361718), Hutton Moor (SE/353735) and Nunwick (SE/ 323747). They are all similar to Thornborough and lie to the south in the same area, but they have been almost obliterated by ploughing.

Scattered across the Yorkshire moors there are a number of relatively small stone circles (and cairn rings) as in Wales. The most convenient area in which to see examples is probably on Ilkley Moor—famous in song and story—where there are at least five circles, (also Bronze Age rock carvings, see p. 111). Ilkley stands on road A65 (Leeds-Skipton) and the moor lies to the south of the town. The best circle is perhaps Horncliffe Circle (SE/134435), strictly an oval, 43 feet across, with forty-six stones still in position. The other possibilities are the Twelve Apostles (SE/126451) and Grubstones (SE/136447), the latter damaged by a quite unnecessary shooting butt.

In Northumberland there are circles at, among other places, Duddo, Goatstones, and Threestone Burn. Duddo circle (NT/ 931437) is about a mile north-west of the village, which can be reached from Berwick along road A6354. There are five large stones still standing. Goatstones (NY/829748) is in wild country, about 3 miles north west of Simonburn, which is itself 10 miles north west of Hexham, (take A6079 and then A6320). It now consists of four stones; the eastern one has a flat top with thirteen cup-engravings (see p. 111) on it. Threestone Burn (NT/972205) stands to the west of South Middleton—turn left off road A697 (Morpeth-Wooler) about 5 miles south of Wooler. Here there are five stones, quite tall, set in a large circle.

In Westmorland—just—there are two circles, 2 miles south of Penrith. Take road A6 south and fork right almost at once along A592; immediately beyond the fork are King Arthur's Round Table and Mayburgh (NY/523284). Both these are hybrids. The former is a henge monument, 300 feet across, with a bank 5 feet high and two entrances, of which one can still be seen in the south-east arc. Mayburgh is a quarter of a mile to the west, 360 feet across, with one entrance to the east, its bank about 10 feet high. The bank has a core of surface stones, and there is a stone at the centre, the survivor of a group of four. It is known that there were also once stones at the centre of the Round Table and at the entrance to both monuments. In Cumberland, see the Carles (NY/292236) just outside Keswick, 110 feet across with thirty-eight stones.

Closely connected in people's minds—and usually rightly so—with stone circles, are avenues and standing stones. As has been noted already, there are conspicuous avenues connected with Avebury and Stanton Drew, of which cursuses and earthen avenues are the ancestors.

The most dramatic stone rows in England are those on Dartmoor. Basically, these stone alignments are of two types. One consists of rows which lead up to burial mounds. There are about sixty of these, most of them short, but a few quite long. An interesting example, comparatively easy to reach, is on the north side of B3212 (Moretonhampstead-Yelverton) 6 miles out of Moretonhampstead and one mile north-west of Warren House Inn (SX/674825). A double row of stones, consisting of fifty pairs of uprights, their size varying from one foot to 6 feet, leads up hill for 540 feet. The northern end is closed by a slab or blocking stone while the southern end, where the row is widest and the stones highest, ends at a low cairn, 20 feet across. Other good rows are at Shovel Down (SX/554824) 3 miles south-west of Chagford, where there are two double rows running from north to south, the more easterly of the two ending at a cairn ring (not a stone circle). Beyond are two more rows.

Not every row leads to a cairn or blocking stone. Some end at a standing stone. Examples of this type are Headland Warren, Challacombe (SX/690809) and Merrivale. Headland Warren is one mile east of Warren House Inn.

At Merrivale (SX/555744) 5 miles out of Tavistock to the south of road A384 (Tavistock-Ashburton) there are two double rows, running east and west. The first to be reached is 596 feet in length, the second 865 feet. Both have blocking stones.

The longest of all such rows are those in the Erme valley. One, at Butterdown Hill (SX/660587) on south Dartmoor to the north of road A38 between Ivybridge and South Brent, runs for 1,250 feet along the crest of the hill. Much longer, though, are the stones at Stall Moor (SX/635644) further up the Erme valley, which run for 2½ miles. It is possible that this monster is the product of two rows, each a giant, which met at the river. Go north-west from Ivybridge along the minor road to Cornwood. The rows begin 3 miles north-east of the village. It is thought that these very long rows were used for ceremonial races. If this is so, they may be considered as an imitation in stone of the cursus.

There are stone rows in other parts of the highland zone, but there is no doubt that the Dartmoor examples are the most rewarding.

As is the case with stone circles and avenues, the erection of isolated standing stones began in Beaker times and continued during the succeeding Bronze Age. The south-west peninsula is particularly rich in standing stones, the largest examples, up to 15 feet in height, being found in Cornwall. The Pipers have already been mentioned. Others stand at Try, Gulval (SW/485350); at Trevennack, Paul (SW/834637); at Trelaw and Pennlyn, St. Buryan (SW/411250); at Kerrow, Zennor. They require more accurate identification than there is room for here, but can be picked out from Ordnance Survey sheet 189.

Outside the South-west and Wales, the most dramatic standing stones are the Devil's Arrows (SE/391666) close to road A1 and just to the south of Boroughbridge. They consist of three stones placed in a north-south line, 200 feet and 370 feet apart. Their heights above ground range from 18 feet to 22½ feet, and they must have been hauled from Knaresborough, 6 or 7 miles to the south-west. The fluting which can be seen at the top of the stones is not man-made, but due to uneven weathering. The Devil's

Arrows are probably part of the same religious complex as the Thornborough and other circles to the north. In a wilder setting they would be greatly romantic, but the main road destroys their splendour.

VI

THE EARLY BRONZE AGE:
1600 to 1300 B.C.

The works of the Beaker folk shade imperceptibly into those of the Bronze Age. The whole structure of 'ages' needs to be—and in some areas is being—dismantled, but in the meantime it provides a usefully rigid frame of reference. In the south of Britain the Bronze Age may be regarded as having lasted for rather more than 1,000 years 1600 to 500 B.C.). A brilliant Early Bronze Age in Wessex (1600 to 1300) was succeeded by a rather humdrum Middle Bronze Age (1300 to 900) and a solid, but still unspectacular Late Bronze Age (900 to 500). Yet in the two later periods important technological advances occurred. The whole period was characterized by a climate drier indeed than at any other time during the last 7,000 years of our history.

The comparatively cut and dried pattern must be constantly qualified. As with all cultural divisions—and this is not peculiar to prehistory, consider the difficulties in the use of such labels as 'Renaissance' or 'Victorian'—there is considerable overlap with, at the beginning, the New Stone Age, and, at the end, the Iron Age. In the Early Bronze Age there was little bronze in use—in early graves only about 5 per cent of the remains are of that metal. The new material was already affecting the scale of activities, but it co-existed alongside the old-fashioned materials, stone and bone. There continued, too, to be great variations in the speed at which new cultures reached different areas and the form they developed when they got there.

During the middle centuries of the second millenium Wessex, almost always in prehistoric times one of the most advanced areas of Britain, experienced a peak of activity and civilization.

The activity seems to have been the consequence of two factors: a localized invasion, and an international trade route. With regard to the first of these, a small war group from Brittany reached Dorset about 1700 B.C. The essential element in this group was a warrior aristocracy which resembled, though faintly and on a lesser scale, the heroic Grecian chieftains described by Homer.

Full of what one archaeologist has characterized as 'barbaric swagger', these men established little principalities here, ruling over the existing inhabitants, the docile peasant farmers, intermarrying with their subjects, and burying their own leaders in individual tombs equipped with an impressive death kit of weapons and luxury goods.

Theirs was an entrepôt wealth. Through Wessex ran the trade route along which those highly-desirable products, Irish and Welsh copper and gold, passed on one stage of the long journey towards their ultimate destination, southern Europe in general and the Mycenean civilization of the eastern Mediterranean in particular.

The easiest route across the peninsula of south-western England skirted Salisbury Plain, linking the Bristol and English Channels. It brought wealth and comparative luxury to these merchant-aristocrats of Wessex, men who had remained in close contact with the areas of France from which they had originally come. Conquest, immigration and trade—a trade that was as much a social as an economic necessity—all played a part in the culture of Wessex at this time. This development was narrowly confined to Wessex itself, together with outlying 'colonies' in East Anglia and South Wales.

By 1500 B.C. the culture was at its height, its most impressive achievement being the rebuilding of Stonehenge in its penultimate, most splendid form, while the surrounding plain was sown ever more thickly with tombs—round barrows and the more specialized Wessex forms, the bell-barrow and the disc barrow. Great men were brought from neighbouring areas to lie at last within this hub of sacred sites (the dagger of one chief is wrapped in sphagnum moss from the New Forest away to the south-east).

Stonehenge III (for Stonehenge I and Stonehenge II see pp. 64–6 and 80–81 respectively) consists of three stages, spanning the years from about 1600 to 1300 B.C. The complex reconstructions and reshufflings seem to have followed very closely on the heels of one another, for 300 years a frenzy of building and rebuilding occupied the attentions and the resources of the area.

In the first reconstruction (Stonehenge IIIa) the unfinished circle of bluestones was removed and in its place was built the great circle of sarsen stones with lintels across the top and the horseshoe of five trilithons within it which together remain today the most obvious features of the site. The new construction was orientated, like its predecessor, towards the midsummer sunrise in the north-east. To create it, more than eighty sarsens were hauled from the Marlborough Downs, 30 miles or more away. At the same time four smaller stones were set up in the circle of the Aubrey holes, and a sarsen stone entrance was erected at the north-east. Of this entrance only one stone remains, the large fallen Slaughter Stone. (Incidentally, recent excavation uncovered here, among other remains, a bottle of port of about the year 1801, which had been buried by a William Cunnington!)

Stonehenge IIIa has been altered and battered about in the course of 3,500 years, but it still possesses a symmetry, a precision, an attention to exact construction, a formal beauty that sets it apart from all the other stone monuments of prehistoric northern Europe.

The stones are carefully dressed; they are held in place by exact mortise and tenon joints; the lintels are curved to conform exactly to the circumference of the circle which they help to create; the geometry of the whole erection is strict.

Everything points to the over-riding supervision of one man, and that a man who was familiar with the sophisticated architecture of the eastern Mediterranean area. To some this may come as an unusual, unlikely suggestion; however, it is not the assumption of one of the many groups of Stonehenge cranks, but is one that on the contrary is today generally accepted by reputable archaeologists. Thus, for instance, J. F. S. Stone writes of Stonehenge as unique in north-western Europe and continues ". . . a unique object postulates a unique event, and I feel sure that we must look to the literate civilizations of the Mediterranean for the inspiration and indeed for the actual execution under the hands and eyes of some trader or mission from that region".[1]

There is specific evidence to support the general theory. Although modern men had been examining Stonehenge closely with care and curiosity for 200 years, it was only in 1953 that for the first time they noticed carved on certain of the stone uprights the faint outlines of bronze axe-heads and of a bronze dagger. The axe heads are of the pattern made in Ireland and exported by

[1] J. F. S. Stone, *Wessex Before the Celts*, (Thames and Hudson, 1958), p. 95.

way of Wessex in the period 1600 to 1400 B.C. The outline of the dagger is even more remarkable, more exciting. Twelve inches long, it is of a type that can be matched from the shaft graves of Mycenae in Greece. One other carving of this type is know in Britain. It was found on a sandstone slab at Badbury in Dorset, and is now in the British Museum. The date of the Mycenean daggers is about 1500 B.C. The carvings help to date the sarsen circle and certainly indicate some sort of connection with the Mediterranean world. With regard to the axes, one of the exact types carved was recovered within 500 yards of Stonehenge.

Stonehenge IIIa was magnificent, yet within a very few years the design was being modified. Perhaps the local inhabitants were dissatisfied with the treatment of their beloved bluestones. About twenty of the discarded bluestones were erected within the sarsen horseshoe in the form of one of the old-fashioned ovals, some of them being dressed to form small imitations of the trilithons. There is evidence, in the form of two concentric circles of holes (the Z and Y holes) outside the sarsen circle that it was intended to put up the rest of the bluestones in two concentric circles, but this was never done.

The whole scheme—which, incidentally, would have resulted in an unbearably cluttered and inartistic construction—was suddenly abandoned and the inner oval of bluestones was taken to pieces. In consequence there is nothing of this half-cock structure that can now be seen, except the never-occupied Z and Y holes.

At once the final reconstruction (Stonehenge IIIc) took place. The bluestone oval was re-arranged as a horseshoe, using nineteen of the largest and most elegant bluestones, with a large pillar of Pembroke sandstone (the 'Altar Stone') placed as a single standing stone within the horseshoe and facing the central sarsen trilithon. The remaining bluestones were set in a circle *within* the great sandstone circle.

And that was the final stage in the long and complex history of Stonehenge, a stage reached by about 1300 B.C. Or rather, it was the final stage in the erection of the sanctuary, for since that date for 3,000 years it has had a mainly unknown story of stones falling down or being removed.

The most recent recorded falls are those of one of the great sarsen trilithons on the west side which fell outwards on 3rd January 1797, "with a very sensible concussion or jarring of the ground" as was noted at the time, and of one of the uprights and lintels of the sandstone circle, close to this trilithon, which fell on 31st

December 1900. These were all re-erected in 1958 by the Ministry of Works.

The effect of the destruction which Stonehenge has suffered has —though one ought not to say so—perhaps in one way been not altogether disastrous. Its most general consequence has been the disappearance of many of the bluestones, so that what one first notices today is largely the remains of Stonehenge IIIa, undoubtedly the 'best' construction.

To help to make clear an admittedly difficult history, it is worth considering what one can now see.

Stand at the centre of Stonehenge. On the ground at your feet lies the so-called Altar Stone, the fallen pillar of Pembrokeshire sandstone from IIIc. Around it are twelve of the original nineteen stones of the bluestone horseshoe (IIIc), eight still standing and four fallen. On two of these bluestones can be seen the remains of projecting tenons, required in the construction of Stonehenge IIIb. Surrounding this horseshoe are the remains of the most immediately impressive structure, the five sarsen trilithons of Stonehenge IIIa of which three now stand. The uprights weigh anything up to 45 tons, increasing in height to the central pair which, including 8 feet below ground level, have a total length of 30 feet.

Outside this complex of Altar Stone, bluestone horseshoe and sarsen horseshoe, are the circles themselves. Still moving outwards, one passes the remains of the bluestone circle, erected in the last period—Stonehenge IIIc. Once there were about sixty stones in this circle, set close together. Twenty stones have survived, of which ten are still standing, rather inconspicuously. They can best be seen in the north-east arc. Outside these remnants stands the other conspicuous feature today, the Sarsen Circle IIIa. Originally there were thirty uprights, capped by thirty lintels. The uprights area bout 20 feet in length, standing 13 feet 6 inches above ground, and weighing about 25 tons, while the lintels weigh about 7 tons each. Seventeen of the uprights stand today, but only six of the lintels are still in position.

Outside the stone circles there is less of obvious grandeur. The Z and Y circles of holes, dug for Stonehenge IIIb, surround the Sarsen Circle, but are not marked. Beyond them one reaches the circle of fifty-six Aubrey Holes, about half of which, on the south side of the complex, are marked in the chalk. These holes date from Stonehenge I. On the circumference of this circle, and overlying it, are two mounds, diametrically opposite one another, and six holes away from these mounds and also diametrically opposite one another are a pair of stones. These make up the four stations, over the significance of which so much heat has been generated.

Outside the Aubrey Holes and stations, are the bank and ditch, also dating from Stonehenge I, broken by the avenue constructed at the time of Stonehenge II and probably marking the track by which the bluestones were hauled up from the River Avon.

Leaving Stonehenge by way of the avenue, one has on one's right a large fallen stone, the Slaughter Stone. The name is modern, the stone—as noted above—probably formed part of a ceremonial gateway (IIIc). Down the avenue, 256 feet from the centre of Stonehenge one reaches the large standing stone, known as the Heel Stone, which must date from Stonehenge I, since the later avenue had to take it into account. Beyond it the avenue leads to the river Avon at West Amesbury.

Throughout written history Stonehenge has, not surprisingly, caught the attention and the imagination of those who have observed it. Within seventy years of the Norman Conquest it was recorded as one of the 'wonders of Britain', and Merlin, King Arthur's wizard, was known to have erected it, by magical methods. Geoffrey of Monmouth (1135) added that the stones had been brought from Ireland by water. In view of the fact that the bluestones *were* brought by water from Pembrokeshire, which lay in the Irish cultural sphere of influence, Geoffrey's statement is either a remarkable example of the persistence of folk-memory or an even more remarkable coincidence.

Henry of Huntingdon, in the same century, wrote that the stones seemed "to hang in the air . . . nor can anyone conceive by what art such great stones have been raised aloft . . .".

Layamon [c. 1200] wrote of the stones:

> Magic power they have.
> Men that are sick
> Fare to that stone;
> And they wash that stone
> And bathe away their evil.

This custom continued until the beginning of the eighteenth century.

In the sixteenth century William Camden, one of the first English archaeologists, was not prepared to "argue and dispute, but rather to lament with much grief, that the authors of so notable a monument are buried in oblivion". He was, however, prepared to consider the theory that the stones were not natural, but a kind of concrete "artificially made of pure sand, and by some gluey and unctuous matter knit and incorporated together".

The poets were not so confident. Sir Philip Sidney wrote that

> neither any eye can count them, nor reason try
> What force them brought to so unlikely ground.

While Samuel Daniel was writing at much the same date and in much the same vein of

> That huge dumb heap, that cannot tell us how
> Nor what, nor whence it is, nor with whose hands
> Nor for whose glory, it was set. . . .
>
> *(Musophilus)*

In the seventeenth century the two great English diarists both visited Stonehenge. On 22nd July 1654, John Evelyn commented "the stone is so exceedingly hard that with all my strength with a hammer could not break a fragment . . .". And that, of course, is one way in which Stonehenge has suffered over the centuries. Indeed, in the early nineteenth century you could still hire a hammer in the village of Amesbury with which to chip off a souvenir—and, if your strength failed, a shepherd would do it for you!

On 11th June 1688, Samuel Pepys visited Stonehenge, and wrote of the stones as "prodigious as any tales I ever heard of them, and worth going this journey to see. God knows what their use was! they are hard to tell [count], but yet may be told. Give the shepherd-woman, for leading our horses, 4d." Pepys, as usual, checking his information by personal inspection.

It was the so-called rational eighteenth century that fastened the druids on to Stonehenge, from which their grip has not yet been entirely loosened. They had, of course, nothing to do with the construction. They may, just conceivably, have used the site in late Iron Age days, but see pp. 146–8.

A rather different line of enquiry has arisen from the fact that Stonehenge appears to embody certain astronomical alignments. The first man to comment in writing on this aspect was Dr. John Smith in 1771. He noted that on 21st June, the longest day, the sun rose over the Heel Stone. The axis of Stonehenge II was certainly arranged to lead towards sunrise on this day. So much is certain. Whether the importance of this sunrise came from the fact that the builders were sun-worshippers, or merely from the necessity of checking an easily-observable date each year, an archaeologist would not be prepared to say. It would seem not unreasonable to assume that the two activities might be closely connected. It should be noted that a point diametrically opposite the entrance, that of the great central trilithon, would mark the point of sunset on the shortest day of the year, 21st December. This may very well have been the more important date, marking the death and rebirth of the year.

Slightly less certain, but reasonably so, are the alignments of the Four Stations on the circumference of the ditch and bank. A line from the centre to the north-east station would mark sunrise on 5th February and 8th November, while sunset over the south-west station would similarly mark 6th May and 8th August. These four dates—5th February, 6th May, 8th August and 8th November —when taken together with the summer and winter solstices and the spring and autumn equinoxes, divide the year into eight approximately equal divisions of about forty-five days each.

So much seems fairly well established. Excited by these align-ments, observers of varying degrees of archaeological expertise, have found many more. Here one must enter a caveat. There are so many stones at Stonehenge that the number of possible align-ments is very large indeed and the possibility of coincidence must be borne in mind.

In my own town the midday sun stands over the park gates and shines directly down the High Street, but it is unlikely that those who put up the gates about 1876 were concerned with this fact. A similar point has been made on a grander scale concerning the Arc de Triomphe. On Napoleon's birthday the sun, observed from the Champs Elysées, sets in the centre of the Arc. Allowing that either the rising or the setting of the sun on this line would be equally remarkable and that these events might coincide with either the birth or death of Napoleon, and remembering that the sun can be seen through the Arc during a whole fortnight, then the odds against a significant position of the sun coinciding with either the birth or death of Napoleon fall to the unimpressive figure of six and a half to one.

With the general point in mind that coincidence of time and space are not necessarily intentional or statistically impressive, one must approach with a certain amount of caution the more exciting theories concerning megalithic circles in general and Stone-henge in particular.

These theories are argued most impressively by G. S. Hawkins, Professor of Astronomy at Boston University, in *Stonehenge*

Decoded (London, 1965) and A. Thom, Emeritus Professor of Engineering Science at Oxford, in *Megalithic Sites in Britain* (Oxford University Press, 1967).

Briefly, Hawkins believes that the slightly mysterious Aubrey Holes "served as a computer" and demonstrates a method by which they might have been used to keep accurate track of the moon and hence to have predicted "the most spectacular eclipses of the moon and the sun", which involves a cycle of nineteen plus nineteen plus eighteen years—a fifty-six-year period which at least coincides with the number of the Aubrey Holes. (The argument is worked out in detail on pages 139–144 of Hawkins book.)

Thom, in his book, examines from a mathematical point of view about 300 megalithic sites and from his measurements deduces the use of right-angled triangles to construct the circles—which are often not circular at all, but egg-shaped. He estimates that these sites are laid out with an inaccuracy of no more than 1 in 1,000 and continues "Whatever we do we must avoid approaching the study with the idea that Megalithic man was our inferior in ability to think" (p. 166). He demonstrates that these circles could have been used for a number of astronomical observations. He also believes that the standard of measurement does not vary from one site to another and from this he deduces a unit of measurement of 2·72 feet (*c.* 82 centimetres) which he christens "a Megalithic yard", possibly derived from a normal pace.

The authors are distinguished men, their arguments are persuasive. Professional archaeologists remain doubtful, and the whole controversy is at the moment a very hot potato indeed. Meanwhile, the traveller, having mastered the argument, can add to his enjoyment by carrying in his car a length of wood 2·72 feet in length and drawing his own conclusions.

Whatever one's opinions, the size of Stonehenge and its precise geometry must inspire one with great respect for those who devised and, in successive phases, reconstructed this unique complex—temple, calendar and observatory.

The traveller, unless he is fortunate in the time of his visit, must take the alignments on trust, but he can see for himself the size of the undertaking. How on earth did the stones get there? One is almost prepared to believe that it was indeed by Merlin's magic that they were erected.

The prodigious labour involved in the construction of prehistoric monuments both here and on the continent is constantly impressive.

Avebury, a 'henge monument'. The remains of the South Circle and Cove can be seen within the Great Circle in the quadrant at the top of the photograph.

Avebury *(above)* Part of the Great Circle, ditch and bank. *(below)* Stukeley's sketch showing the destruction of one of the stones.

In Brittany there is a single stone the original height of which was 65 feet, while at Carnac, also in Brittany, over 1,000 large stones are arranged in ten parallel avenues stretching for 3½ miles. In Ireland there exists a single capstone weighing 100 tons. In Scotland Gordon Childe has estimated that in the cairns of Caithness, although the individual stones are small, there is in each one enough material—about 8,000 tons—to build five fair-sized parish churches.

The effort required to build prehistoric monuments is implicit also, though less obviously, in the huge quantities of earth shifted to make an earthen long barrow, to lay out a cursus, to construct the great bank and ditch at Avebury or to raise the huge artificial hill at Silbury. All these were the creation of people who have left virtually no sign of their worldly settlements.

How were these feats of engineering carried out? What was the social imperative that drove forward the groups involved in these vast co-operative efforts?

The tasks were great, but they were not beyond the power of primitive civilizations—one does not have to bring in, as some do, engineers from Atlantis or Venus.

Evidence is available from more modern times as to the effort required. In the early nineteenth century the French authorities found it necessary to move a megalithic capstone when reconstructing a road. They employed a team of eighteen oxen and rollers over a metre in circumference. Prehistoric man would have used human beings in place of oxen.

More recently, Thor Heyerdahl, investigating the labour involved in raising the colossal stone heads that stand mysteriously rooted in the earth of Easter Island in the Pacific, demonstrated that these could be lifted into position by a team of twelve islanders in eighteen days.

In England the stone circle at Avebury was examined in the 1930s and in the course of this examination one of the standing stones was re-erected. It took thirteen men five days to do this.

Of all the feats of construction, one of the most impressive, and the one that has been most carefully examined, was that of the building of Stonehenge. Here there are problems of transport, as well as problems of erection.

The bluestones must have come from the Prescelly Mountains in Pembrokeshire. Various routes have been suggested. The shortest would be across country, passing the Severn in the neighbourhood of Gloucester, a total distance of about 180 miles. The longest route is by water around Land's End to Christchurch in Hampshire and then up the Salisbury Avon. Neither is now considered probable. The first is over difficult country, the second includes some very treacherous stretches of water.

The most probable route runs from the Prescellys to Milford Haven, then by sea, hugging the coast, to Avonmouth on the east side of the Bristol Channel. From there the stones could be taken up the Bristol Avon and its tributary, the Frome, overland to a point near Warminster, then by water again along the Wylye and the Salisbury Avon to the point where the avenue reaches the river near West Amesbury, and finally up the route now marked by the avenue to the site itself, a total distance of about 240 miles.

Milford Haven was almost certainly the point of departure. The sandstone Slaughter Stone comes from that point, while the coast route along South Wales was already in use as a trade route for the transport of stone axes.

Down to Milford Haven the stones would be dragged on sledges. In the water they would be loaded onto rafts or slung between rafts, canoes or skin boats for the intermediate water-borne stages, and finally dragged up the avenue to the site.

The sarsen stones were moved from the Marlborough Downs near Avebury to Stonehenge entirely overland, by a route that probably ran by way of Bishops Cannings, Redhorn Hill and Robin Hood Ball, to Stonehenge, a distance of over 30 miles.

In 1954 the B.B.C. helped to carry out some experiments on the Avon near Stonehenge. A concrete copy of one of the bluestones was put on a platform made from three canoes, based on prehistoric examples. It was found that four schoolboys could pole this contraption upstream. The canoes drew only 9 inches of water. At sea a raft, though with greater draft, would have been more stable. On land it was found that it required thirty-two boys to pull the concrete copy, now loaded on a sledge, up a gradient of 1 in 14. If the sledge was pulled over rollers, instead of directly over the ground, the reduction in friction made it possible for fourteen boys to move the load. Nevertheless, the advantage of cutting land haulage to a minimum is very clear. The transport of the heaviest sarsen may easily have required 500 men at the steepest places, while the journey from the Marlborough Downs and back again would have taken a fortnight.

A point often overlooked is the effort involved in dressing the stones. A comparison of the undressed sarsens at Avebury with the accurately shaped lintels and uprights at Stonehenge makes quite clear what a vast amount of labour was involved. Experiments have shown that maul-pounding—the method employed—can remove perhaps 6 cubic inches in an hour. Professor Atkinson has estimated that the construction of Stonehenge involved the removal of perhaps 3 million cubic inches by this method.

Finally, having been transported and shaped, the stones had to be lifted into position. The largest sarsens at Stonehenge weigh about 45 tons—the largest single stone in the Great Pyramid is thought to weigh perhaps 15 tons. The method employed was to dig a foundation pit with one side sloping. The stone was rolled forward until its base lay over the hole. The top was then levered up. Timber packing was inserted to act as a fulcrum between the stone and the surface of the ground, and this wooden pile was gradually raised until the stone could be pulled upright and the sloping side of the pit wedged with stones. It seems likely that a gang of 200 men would be required to raise a stone in this way. One's amazement increases when one remembers that it was not a question of merely raising each stone to a vertical position, but also of ensuring that its final height and orientation conformed to very exact mathematical standards.

The lintels were raised into position by building a platform around the uprights and raising this a little at a time, lifting the lintel onto each fresh level by means of levers. Finally, when the lintels were at a slightly higher level than the tops of the uprights they were worked sideways until they could be dropped into position, their mortise fitting exactly over the tenon cut in the upright.

These, it is considered, are the only possible methods by which the sarsen circle and the trilithons could have been erected.

Stonehenge and other megalithic monuments imply a considerable degree of engineering accuracy and a powerful social need. Opinions differ as to whether the engineering skill was local or foreign. As has been seen, there are good grounds for thinking that Stonehenge IIIa, at least, was the product of a Mediterranean mind.

What motives provided the psychological driving force? Clearly even the most insignificant long barrow could not have been erected for a purely local or individual whim. The available resources and technical skill needed to raise the greater monuments are, for their day, a reputable archaeologist has suggested, comparable with the effort expended by modern man in the exploration of space. One would be hard put to it to give due weight to the different impulses which have in the twentieth century led man to the moon. For our Neolithic, Beaker and Bronze Age ancestors pride and fear, rivalry and experiment were, no doubt, mingled with religious, agricultural and political requirements.

It is at least clear that the planning, alignment and construction of Stonehenge implies great powers of co-ordination and a considerable reservoir of manpower. These in turn must have rested on a stable social structure, itself the product of economic security.

The Early Bronze Age culture of Wessex was stable and rich. The richness is inferred from the material remains found in the graves of chieftains. Gold is everywhere. Gold in a variety of forms. The objects are not of Irish design though they are presumably of Irish gold. Beaten into thin—sometimes very thin—sheets, they include gold mace heads and lozenge-shaped pectoral plates now in the Dorchester Museum; gold inlay; gold-mounted pendants of the type to be seen in the Devizes Museum; gold-plated beads and cones; crescents of gold 8 inches in diameter probably worn on the chest (lunulae) like the ones in Truro Museum; gold-mounted amber discs; golden ear-rings; and a most beautiful gold cup found at Rillaton, south-east of Bodmin, and now in the British Museum. The cup, only $3\frac{1}{4}$ exquisite inches in height, is similar to ones recovered from the royal graves of the sixteenth-century Mycenaean civilization, 1,500 miles away as the crow flies—the same graves in which an Irish bronze halberd of the period has been found, evidence of trading contacts in the reverse direction.

This golden shower is as unexpected and magnificent as it is unprecedented. Nothing has prepared the way for these riches, nothing develops from them.

Nor is this all. There are objects of amber. They are of local design, and therefore the material must have been imported in its raw state from the European source of amber, the Baltic region. It was then worked up in Britain into beads, spacing plates on necklaces, discs and cups such as the one found at Clandon carved from a single lump of this rare, magical substance, or the one made of red amber and holding almost half a pint that was found at Hove. Hove lies outside the Wessex area, but goods from Wessex have been found much farther afield. An amber necklace was discovered in far-away Orkney at the Knowes of Trotty.

More remarkable still, beads of faience have been dug up from about forty graves in Wessex. Now faience was an oriental luxury product, probably first produced in Mesopotamia, but later manufactured in Egypt. It is a composite artificial material, usually made in two stages. First a moulded core of finely powdered quartz was heated until the quartz fused and then the resulting bead was glazed with a coloured slip, normally a blue or green colour derived from copper compounds. Alternatively, the slip was sometimes mixed with the quartz and the bead fired in one operation.

About 1500 B.C. faience beads from the eastern Mediterranean began to find their way to places as far apart as central Africa and Siberia. The trade routes were long and dangerous—an interesting theory is that if the probable voyage of the legendary Jason and his Argonauts is plotted it follows one of the routes of faience distribution.

In England there is a heavy concentration in Wessex of a type of faience bead, the segmented bead, produced in Egypt between the years 1450 and 1360 B.C. The two routes by which this specialized product reached Britain were up the Danube and then down the Rhine, or alternatively across southern France by way of the Carcassonne gap to the estuary of the Garonne and then coastwise to Brittany and the south coast of England.

From Brittany itself the Wessex chieftains received beautiful ceremonial axes of jadeite which may have been *douceurs* given by Breton traders to ensure their receiving a favourable share of the rarities that were passing through Wessex.

Thus Irish gold and copper, Cornish tin, Baltic amber *objets de vertu* from Greece and Egypt and Brittany—all found their way for a comparatively brief space of time to a Wessex which had become an important *entrepôt*.

All the evidence points to the existence of "an heroic aristocracy amassing unproductive weapons and luxury articles"[1] supported by the unrecorded labours of a semi-nomadic society. Northern Europe in general was enjoying a brief trading summer. In continental Europe the interchange of products is neatly demonstrated by a find from the province of Drenthe in the Netherlands, where beads of tin, amber and faience are united in one necklace.

Behind all this there lay the activities of the bronzesmiths themselves. Bronze, a mixture of tin and copper, was worked in two, largely complementary, ways. Because of its low melting-point it can be easily cast and the casting of objects in moulds became highly competent. In the most complicated method the object was first moulded in wax. Then the wax was enclosed in clay and the clay heated. This hardened the clay and also melted the wax which could be poured out and the molten metal poured in—the *cire*

[1] J. F. S. Stone, *Wessex Before the Celts*, (Thames and Hudson, 1958), p. 121.

perdue process. Bronze can also be worked by cold hammering and this method was used for constructing flanges and flattening rivet heads, for hardening cutting edges, for producing sheet metal and applied decoration.

Yet for all their riches, their technical competence and their cosmopolitan connections, the Wessex men have left hardly a trace of their settlements or of their daily life. As already noted, the mildness of the climate and the semi-nomadic nature of their agriculture both militated against the construction of strongly-built, permanent settlements. Once again, the picture which the archaeologist paints is narrowly limited by the range of colours at his disposal.

Death and religion dominate the scene, while of the where and how of daily life we know scarcely anything. Flimsy settlements may have been built in the temporarily accessible river valleys. Later centuries of farming in historical times in those same valleys are not the least potent reason why prehistorians so often find themselves dealing with hilltop sites.

Death and religion. Stonehenge may stand for religion, while death is represented by the round barrows which pepper southern England.

The round barrow first reached Britain in Beaker times (see p. 74). In this, as in so much else, there is continuity between that period and the Early Bronze Age. The round barrow proved such a socially acceptable form of tomb, at least for the ruling classes, that it persisted throughout the Middle and Late Bronze Ages (1300 to 500 B.C.), even persisted to a limited extent for another 1,000 years (500 B.C. to A.D. 650) throughout the Iron Age, the Roman occupation and on into Saxon times. Seldom can a tomb-form have had such lasting popularity. Its final examples lie outside the scope of this book, but those interested should see the Saxon barrow in the grounds of Taplow Court, Buckinghamshire (SU/911822), and the finds from that barrow which are now in the British Museum.

With such a chronological spread, statements about round barrows are likely to require qualification, and the following is no more than a rough guide.

In the South-west Peninsula there are over 800 round barrows in Cornwall and over 500 in Devon. In Wessex of the 6,000 still visible about 4,000 were constructed between the end of the Beaker period and the start of the Late Bronze Age—a period of roughly 700 years. This was the peak time of round barrow buildings and the favourite shape was that of the bowl barrow (see p. 74). Ninety per cent are of this type.

From the grave goods one can deduce the wealth of the Wessex period—at least in so far as its rulers are concerned. Those on whose bent backs society rested remain—as usual—unknown.

Round barrows are not peculiar to Britain. In Wessex, however, there developed specialized shapes, unknown on the continent. It is possible, though not proved, that these derived from that other native creation, the henge monument.

The surviving numbers of these specialized types are:

bell barrows	245
disc barrows	149
saucer barrows	63
pond barrows	53

The bell barrow consists of a carefully shaped conical mound surrounded by a flat platform which is in turn bounded by an accurately placed, exactly cut, ditch. The ditch clearly has a ritual significance and is not merely the area from which material has been obtained for the central mound.

In the disc barrow the mound is reduced to a small central pimple, the platform between it and the surrounding ditch is correspondingly larger, and there is an outer bank. For the saucer barrow the area within the bank and ditch is uniformly raised and the central mound has virtually disappeared. Lastly, the pond barrow resembles a shallow inverted bowl barrow, consisting of a gentle hollow enclosed by an outer bank and, occasionally, a ditch.

An interesting feature of these variant forms is that there seems to have been a sex difference involved. Bell barrows have been found to contain normally the remains of males, while disc and saucer barrows usually hold the remains of females.

Very little is known about pond barrows. They occur in two main areas, Salisbury Plain and south Dorset. In the latter area one example has been carefully excavated at Sheep Down, Winterbourne Steepleton (finds in the British Museum). The inner area had been paved with a floor, 7 inches thick, of packed flints. There were a number of cremations from the Middle Bronze Age, but these were later than the original barrow and it is possible that pond barrows, though connected with death, did not themselves contain burials.

There are a few hybrids. Multiple barrows occur where two—or, rarely, three—barrows are surrounded by a single enclosing ditch, the assumption being that these twins or triplets were erected as a group.

For all types of barrow one must remember that the burial itself was almost always below ground level and not, as one tends to imagine it, at the centre of gravity of the mound.

Barrows may be found in isolation or, more commonly, in groups which the archaeologist is surely justified in calling cemeteries. Some of these cemeteries seem to have grown up around a founder's grave of the late Beaker period—a pattern that must lead one to speculate on the relationship between the Beaker chiefs and their descendants or supplanters. Areas of special sanctity—for instance Avebury and Stonehenge—attracted very large numbers of barrows. At the latter site 310 barrows are clustered within an area of 12 square miles, an average density of twenty-five burials per square mile.

A few barrows have been found on low-lying ground, but in general, whether singly or in clumps, they are superbly sited on the skyline. Since the most dramatic horizon is usually not the crest of a hill, the successful choice of a position ensuring maximum visibility was deliberate, difficult, sophisticated. It also implies that the areas involved must have been clear of forests and thick undergrowth at the time when the barrows were raised.

In the earlier round barrows the corpse was buried uncremated, as in the Beaker period, usually in a contracted position. There is evidence that the body was sometimes tied in this position with cords, or pushed into a bag. In a few burials, less than 10 per cent, the body was lying at full length. It is supposed that these may be the bodies of those of such a high social position that they had been accustomed, in life, to sleep extended on beds and not curled up like everybody else.

In a few cases the head only was buried, and there is at least one example of the body being buried without its head. Normally, though, the whole corpse was placed, below ground level, at the centre of the barrow, sometimes enclosed in a stone-lined chest or a wooden coffin. One or two burials are, by Bronze Age standards, very deep indeed—5 or 6 feet below ground level—and are covered with a heavy stone slab. An attractive theory is that these graves contain the remains of people whose possible return as ghosts was regarded as being particularly undesirable!

The vast majority of these burials are single, but in a number of barrows a man and a woman have been buried together, and sometimes there is also a child. Occasionally the bones show evidence of rickets. A number of skulls have been found that have been trepanned, a circular piece of bone having been removed from the skull. This in itself is interesting, but the startling fact is that there is no doubt that sometimes the patient recovered, for new bone has grown around the edge of the cut skull. The question immediately arises, how was the patient kept calm during these delicate and apparently successful operations? The answer would appear to be that use was made of massive doses of vegetable drugs, or of hypnosis, or of a combination of both.

Quite soon, by about 1500 B.C., cremation had returned as the dominant ritual. It is unknown what social forces operated to bring about this emotionally important reversal of practice, but it may have been due to the influence of native women who had intermarried with the invaders and persuaded them to adopt the old form of burial, since the evidence indicates that in the early stages of the change-over it was the women who were the more often cremated.

After cremation the ashes, now reduced to a handful about the size of a grapefruit, were buried in a pot, or sometimes wrapped in cloth. Fragments of these cloths provide some of the earliest examples in Britain of woven material.

The widespread adoption of cremation had two incidental consequences. One was contemporary: large amounts of timber were required for the funeral pyres and this must have encouraged the deforestation of many areas. The other consequence is archaeological: cremation results in the disappearance of much that would, if it had survived, have provided useful evidence about the conditions of Bronze Age life.

The raising of a barrow was itself a ritual series of actions and not a mere bit of digging. The remains were interred and the exact spot marked by a small cairn or mound covered with the turf cut from what was to be the surrounding ditch. Next, earth from this ditch was carefully heaped to make the final shape, being supplemented when necessary by supplies from elsewhere. There is evidence that different materials were sometimes deliberately arranged in layers and that, in chalkland areas, the completed barrow was covered with a gleaming white casing of chalk. One wonders if it was kept scoured for hundreds of years or whether weeds and grasses were soon allowed to cloak, slowly but inevitably, the pure white tomb.

Round barrows were normally intended originally for one cere-mony, but many of them have in fact been used several times, so that a barrow may now contain a series of interments extending over a period of perhaps 2,000 years. Some were even re-used by the Saxons, 400 or 500 years after the life of prehistoric Britain had been brought to an end by the arrival of the Roman legions.

An extreme example of the invasion of a round barrow is at Latch Farm, Christchurch. Here a round barrow contained the remains of three bodies, presumably those for which the barrow was originally raised—but it also held the remains of no less than *eighty-seven* later cremations which had been inserted in the sur-rounding ditch and platform, most of them on the south side.

In some cemeteries the various main types of barrow are all represented. A visit to one of these groups is an economical way of collecting examples of the different types and also of learning to recognize the characteristic profiles of each.

Good groups for these purposes exist at Snail Down (SU/220520), Normanton (SU/115413) and Winterbourne Stoke (SU/101417), all in Wiltshire. Snail Down lies about a mile to the south-west of road A342, between Ludgershall and Everleigh. Finds are in Devizes Museum. It is War Department property, but can usually be visited. Although it is getting badly damaged, it is still worth seeing.

Normanton lies about half-a-mile to the south of Stonehenge. Take a path south from road A303. Again finds are in Devizes Museum. Here there are bowl barrows, disc barrows, bell barrows (including a twin) and saucer-barrows, twenty-six in all. Notice especially Bush Barrow, which contained the splendid burial of a Wessex chieftain. He was buried extended and clothed, on his chest was a lozenge-shaped sheet of gold, while his belt was fastened with a gold-plated hook-and-eye. There were three daggers in leather-lined wooden sheaths, one of which had a pommel decorated with a pattern made by hundreds of gold pins. There was a bronze axe wrapped in cloth, the remains of a shield, and a sceptre or ceremonial mace.

Winterbourne Stoke is close by, $1\frac{1}{2}$ miles west of Stonehenge, in the north-east angle between A303 and A360. There are twenty-six round barrows here of various types, including a very clear disc barrow, and a long barrow.

A cemetery outside the Wiltshire area can be seen at Farway (SY/163970–SY/172933) in East Devon. Take road A376 south from Honiton and after 3 miles turn left along B3174. The barrows lies on the ridge of Greensand along which this road runs. There are between fifty and sixty, all of them of the bowl type, on both sides of the road and lying particularly thickly at Roncombe Gate. Some interesting finds are in Exeter Museum, including cups, with handles carved from Dorset shale, and a bone toggle.

In many round barrows of the Early Bronze Age the comparatively large Beaker now gives place to a much smaller cup only about 1½ inches to 3 inches in size. These are usually labelled 'pigmy' or—more debatably—'incense' cups. Their outside is often decorated, and sometimes covered with nobbles. Occasionally, as exemplified in the Normanton cup in Devizes Museum, the cup itself looks suspiciously like a minuscule model of Stonehenge.

Reference has already been made to the stone slab found at Badbury Barrow with carvings of axes and daggers on it similar to those found at Stonehenge. Another slab of almost equal interest found in association with a barrow in southern England is that from Pool Farm in Somerset. Here the stone is marked with the engravings of six human feet. It is well displayed in Bristol Museum—a most evocative sight, bringing one almost in touch with the owners of those feet.

VII

THE MIDDLE AND LATE BRONZE AGES:
1300 to 500 B.C.

If the rest of mainland Britain—Ireland, as always, was a law unto itself—never achieved the cosmopolitan heights of the Wessex culture, it nevertheless had, perhaps, its revenge. When the Wessex society declined about 1300 B.C., the cultures that had developed in other areas became dominant in Wessex also.

What had happened to Wessex? It had lost its market. Significantly, it was about this time that the Minoan civilization of the eastern Mediterranean area collapsed, perhaps at least partly a consequence of the great volcanic explosion which destroyed the island of Thera about 1350 B.C. The destruction and the tidal waves that accompanied this disaster may have been the germ from which grew the legend of Atlantis, a great civilization sunk beneath the ocean, the legend that the priests of Egypt told to Solon in the sixth century B.C.

More prosaically, the cause may be seen in the opening-up of the deep copper deposits of the eastern Alpine area, an opening-up which made unnecessary the long trading links with the copper-producing areas of the British Isles. Whatever the cause, the British metal trade slumped. The economic structure that had made possible Stonehenge III, the golden offerings and the beads of Egyptian faience, broke down.

The glory had departed. The adjectives used to describe the Middle Bronze Age in Wessex by archaeologists include such words as 'uneventful', 'uninteresting', 'monotonous', 'drab'. Partly, of course, it is a matter of contrast. A period twice as long as the Early Bronze Age with no gold, no fancy barrows, no Stonehenge III. Instead, the universal adoption of cremation, with its tendency to reduce the amount of archaeological evidence, a straight run of standard bowl barrows, the simple food vessel and the even more elementary collared urn, a continuing absence of settlement sites.

Into the vacuum left by the collapse of the Wessex culture there flowed from surrounding areas types of pottery and, presumably, ways of life that had established themselves outside Wessex. These had developed in the Early Bronze Age, and it is in many ways convenient to regard areas beyond Wessex as possessing a fairly uniform pattern from 1600 to about 900 B.C.

In those areas the Beaker culture was gradually superseded by the Food Vessel culture (1600 to 1300/1000 B.C.). Its origins remain shadowy, as does its structure, but it probably arose from the interaction of Beaker folk, new immigrants from Spain, and Secondary Neolithic (Peterborough) natives. It flourished in Ireland, Scotland and Wales, while in England it was especially strong in Northumberland, Durham, Yorkshire and the Peak District. The various Food Vessel groups played an important role as middlemen in the Early Bronze Age trade between Ireland and continental Europe.

The Food Vessel which has given these people their name stands typically about 6 inches high and may be as much as 6 inches in diameter at the mouth, narrowing to about half that figure at the base, which is flat. The decoration consists of regular patterns made in the clay with a square-toothed comb or a length of cord and arranged in horizontal rows. Sometimes small lugs were added —a new feature—but in general this simple type continued almost unchanged for at least 300 years. The Food Vessel, like the Beaker, served as a container of food or drink for the use of the dead in the after-life.

Like the Beaker folk too, the Food Vessel people herded sheep and cultivated barley, wove cloth and fastened their clothes with buttons. Sometimes they buried their dead in wooden canoes, cut from a single tree trunk. Ear-rings were fashionable and the women often dressed their hair in the form of a bun held in place by long bone pins. Of the grave goods only about 5 per cent are bronze—ear-rings, daggers, sewing awls, that type of thing. Characteristic, though comparatively rare, are elaborate crescentic necklaces made of plates of jet or Kimmeridge (Dorset) shale arranged in graduated rows.

The areas in which to see the Food Vessel culture at its most pure are in the highland zone.

Some of the most interesting remains have been found in Yorkshire. Often the barrows contain multiple burials. Quernhow Barrow, north of Ripon, was destroyed when the Great North Road was 'improved' in 1949. In the course of its destruction there was uncovered a whole series of ritual pits, cremations, food vessels in hollows, heaps of sand and cobbles, the whole covered by what had appeared to be a perfectly normal, if exceptionally large (100 feet in diameter) round barrow.

At Gristhorpe, on the cliffs between Scarborough and Filey, an oak coffin was found, made from a split oak tree. The dimensions, 7½ feet long, 3 feet 3 inches wide at the head and 2 feet 10 inches at the foot, compare interestingly with those of a modern coffin. Within lay the extended skeleton of a man, 6 feet tall, whose body had been wrapped in a skin, fastened on the breast with a pin of bone. The finds from this barrow are in the Scarborough Museum.

Gristhorpe is by the sea, Loose Howe (NZ/703008) on the Yorkshire moors, yet the burial customs were clearly much the same in each place. The Barrow is to the east of the road over Rosedale Moor, about 3 miles north-west of Rosedale Abbey. There was an oak coffin with a wooden lid from which, when the diggers reached it, water poured out. This water had, fortunately, helped to preserve the contents. A man's body had been bedded on straw and rushes, pillowed on more straw. Some pieces of cloth and leather had survived. There was also a bronze knife placed, as in life, by the left hip, and a quantity of hazel nuts. Beside the coffin there was a 9-foot dugout canoe, with beaked prow and a place for a stern-board to provide stability. The bark had been left on the wood as a form of waterproofing. The surviving fragments of clothing indicated that the man was buried in a woven tunic fastened with buttons, and was wearing leather shoes topped by cloth puttees to protect his shins from rough undergrowth. The finds are now in the British Museum.

At Butterwick the body of a man had been placed at the bottom of a 6-feet-deep pit. His right hand still held the horn haft of a bronze knife which had once been housed in a wooden sheath of which only a little dust remained, while—an interesting juxtaposition—upon the new metal weapon had been laid one of the old-fashioned flint knives. The tunic had decayed completely, but its buttons, one of sandstone and five of jet, lay more or less in their original positions. A bronze axe with traces of its 2-foot wooden helve was at the man's waist.

At Folkton three strange objects were recovered from the grave of a child about 5 years of age. These were three drums of solid chalk, each about 5 inches in diameter and rather less than that in height. They had apparently been carefully arranged so that one was touching the child's head and two were by the hips. Each drum had been beautifully carved in low relief. The patterns round the greater part of the sides are arrangements of triangles and diamonds shaded with criss-cross lines, reminiscent of those on Beaker pots. On one side of each drum, though, there is something unusual, a stylized face—only a matter of three lines and two dots, almost an ideogram, but at the same time completely descriptive. This was originally a Continental decoration, found particularly in southern Europe. Finally, the tops of the drums are ornamented with a pattern of concentric circles, which may echo the cup-and-ring markings of the northern highlands.

Stare as one will at these mysterious little objects, now in the British Museum, they do not give up their secret. They seem too elaborate, too ritualistic, to have been the child's toys. Surely they are full of strong magic; certainly they are unique in England.

The cup-and-ring markings referred to above are not uncommon on the Pennine moors. They consist of hollows, usually shallower than a hemisphere, pecked out of stone slabs and sometimes surrounded with a pecked ring. Occasionally there are other markings. They usually occur in groups and without any apparent reference to burials, but they have been found associated with Food Vessel graves. Engravings of the same type occur in Spain and Portugal, this being one of the reasons for connecting Food Vessel immigrants with that part of Europe.

Cup-and-ring markings are common in Ireland, where continuous lines often link them into patterns; in England they are most easily found in Northumberland and in the North and West Ridings of Yorkshire, particularly in the last-named of these areas on the moors that lie between the rivers Aire and Nidd.

The carvings are usually rather inaccessible, but for an active traveller their very loneliness makes them worth a visit. Ilkley Moor is one of the richest districts.

The Ilkley carvings lie south of road A65 (Leeds-Skipton), clustered in two areas (SE/086472 and SE/132463), both of them a little above the 1,000-feet contour. For the less energetic, there is a carved stone in the park opposite St. Margaret's Church in Ilkley itself, and there are casts of the best moor carvings in Leeds Museum.

Another good group, reasonably accessible, lies on Snowdon Carr about 4 miles north-west of Otley, itself almost half-way between Ilkley and Leeds. In the North Riding at Hinderwell Beacon over 150 carved stones were found piled over a Food Vessel grave. Farther north, still in Northumberland, a group can be seen in the area of Dod Law Camps (NU/004318). The Camps, earthworks perhaps later than the stones, are on the moor to the east of road A6111 (Wooler-Berwick) about 2 miles north of Wooler and before one reaches Doddington.

Related fairly closely to the Food Vessels are the Collared Urns. These were made, though, by a distinct group of people. They can be regarded as an enlarged food vessel and have been described as looking like a large flower-pot. They are more traditional in design than the Food Vessels, less influenced by Beaker and other patterns, more akin to the old native Peterborough traditions. They outlasted the Food Vessels, continuing more or less unchanged until about 1000 B.C. By 1200 B.C. the custom of cremation had become general and the urn which had in life served as a container for food and drink, now became in death a coffin.

It would appear that Collared Urn people colonized eastern Scotland, perhaps moving north from Yorkshire, where their rather uninformative barrows lie near the passes through Wharfedale, Airedale and the Calder valley. Within these barrows the ashes were put into the urn which was then capped with a stone or with another urn, inverted. There was very little in the way of grave goods—a copper knife damaged by fire or a solitary bead.

Exceptionally, there was a fraction more, as at Blackheath Cross, near Todmorden. Here a number of burials were enclosed within a ring cairn. In one there was a pigmy cup, in another four faience beads. The evidence indicates trading connections with the Wessex people. It seems likely that the most valuable object the north could have supplied in exchange would have been jet, which was certainly prized in the south.

The cultures described above were also established in Scotland and Wales. A detailed account lies outside the limits of this book, but a few generalizations may be worth making.

In Scotland the Food Vessel culture established itself in the south-west, in Argyll, Bute, the Clyde Valley and along the south-west coast. In this coastal area there have been found the largest number of faience beads outside Wessex itself.

In North Wales Wessex influence is greater than in South

Arbor Low, a 'henge monument'. The remains of a round barrow can be seen adjoining the right-hand (southern) entrance.

The Carles, Castlerigg, a dramatic stone circle of uncertain date but probably Bronze Age.

Stonehenge, looking north-west. Near the centre of the photograph are two stones of the bluestone horseshoe. Outside these are the trilithons of the sarsen horseshoe. Part of the bluestone circle is on the right and beyond it is the best-preserved arc of the sarsen circle. Projecting tenons can be seen on some of the stones.

Wales, and there a few faience beads have been found. Anglesey, though, came under Irish influence. In South Wales the food vessels are of Irish origin and are usually connected with crema- tions, a feature not typical of mainland Britain. Taken together, this evidence suggests cultural connections between Wessex and south-west Scotland by way of North Wales, while a rather different culture, centred on the Irish Sea, united Ireland and southern Wales, particularly the south-west coast; coastal Glamorganshire on the other hand came under the influence of the Beaker culture of Lowland Britain. A noteworthy discovery made when excavating a cairn at Simondston, Bridgend, Glamor- ganshire, was that in the fifteenth century B.C. coal had been used together with wood in the construction of the funeral pyre—a very early instance of its use.

In North Wales there is one new and interesting feature—the existence of so-called boiling mounds. These are large grass mounds containing only burnt stones and wood ash, found in Anglesey and along the north coast as far as Conway—areas subject to Irish influence. It is thought that they are the remains of hunters' cooking camps. Basically, these consisted of a pit for heating stones and a trough for boiling food. In Ireland an ex- periment was performed in 1953 at a reconstructed mound of this type. The trough took about 100 gallons of water. The stones were heated in the pit until they were red-hot, a process which took about an hour. They were then dropped into the water until after a further half-hour the temperature had been raised to boiling-point. A ten-pound leg of mutton was then put in the water which was kept boiling by the use of more stones for three hours and forty minutes. It is said that the meat was perfectly cooked.

In Lowland Britain the Middle Bronze Age saw developments in metal-working and farming. Bronze, which had really been rather rare in the Early Bronze Age, became more usual, and new types of weapon were developed in the south, types that eventu- ally came to be manufactured also in the highland zone.

Three of the types most likely to be encountered by the museum wandered are the palstave, the socketed spearhead and the rapier. The palstave represented an improved form of axe head. The problem had always been that of fixing the head to the shaft so that it was firm and so that the haft did not work up along the blade. In the palstave that part of the axe-head which fitted into the split shaft was provided with double flanges along each edge.

H

These gave added stability. At the same time a stop-ridge was cast across the head below the cutting edge to prevent the wooden haft moving towards the blade. Later, a loop was cast on the lower edge of the axe-head so that it could be made even firmer by lashing it to the axe handle, and eventually two loops appeared, one on either edge (the double-looped palstave).

The rapier was really a relatively short thrusting sword, not more than 2 feet in length with a sharp point and a blade that was only moderately narrow, it did not remotely resemble the modern rapier. The socketed spearhead did for the spear what the palstave did for the axe. The socket gripped the wooden shaft and the sides of the socket were often equipped with loops so that the head could be bound onto the shaft. These three types were all cast in two-piece moulds of wood, stone or clay fitted together accurately and bound with cords.

Farming changed more slowly, and the changes are not so obvious as in man-made objects like pots or metalware. What follows is a highly generalized description of farming during the millenium which extends from the Beaker folk to the Late Bronze Age—say from 1800 to 800 B.C.

Throughout, barley was the staple crop, though a little wheat was still grown. From the earlier years of the Bronze Age crescent-shaped flint sickle blades have survived, their butts indicating that they were fixed at right angles into wooden handles. During the Middle Bronze Age a vastly more efficient metal sickle began to come into use. After reaping, the corn was threshed on smooth earthen threshing-floors of the type that can still be seen in use today in, for instance, Spain. About a third of the crop was kept back and stored for use as seed-corn in the following season. The remainder was made into bread and beer. The bread corn was ground in saddle querns, in which a convex pillow-shaped upper stone was rubbed by hand backwards and forwards across the surface of a concave-shaped lower stone, the grain lying between the two.

The type of animal kept varied somewhat with the local conditions. In general the commonest domesticated animal was the sheep. Pigs, too, were numerous and so were oxen. The large ox *(Bos primegenius)* was eventually replaced by a smaller, shorter-horned variety *(Bos longifrons)*. A small horse appeared on the scene. It stood about twelve hands high and was like a Shetland or Exmoor pony—animals which may be its descendants. Dogs were kept, animals with long legs, short backs and small heads of much the same indeterminate breed as those kept in Neolithic times at Windmill Hill *(Canis familiaris palustris)*.

For the earlier part of the period, shallow pits and rows of stakeholes suggest the footings for simple huts or even low tents of the type found today in North Africa. The Beaker people, as already noted, certainly lived in the already three-quarter-filled ditches of the old Neolithic causewayed camps, littering the upper levels of those ditches with their pots and their rubbish. Some regard this as evidence of ceremonial visits to half-misunderstood constructions, but from the casual nature of the remains it seems much more likely that the Beaker squatters simply saw the ditches as convenient depressions that would save them a lot of digging.

At Durrington Walls there has been found along the southern side a line of fifty-eight post-holes with offsets, together with a vast quantity of pig bones, which suggests that there was some form of farming settlement there. In Hampshire archaeologists came upon a probable pit-trap for catching game. Eight feet six inches deep, it certainly trapped a terrier during the excavations.

It is only after the decline of the rich Wessex culture that any firm evidence is available for the existence of what might today be regarded as farms.

One of the best-investigated sites is that at Shearplace Hill (SY/640986). Turn east off road A37 (Dorchester-Yeovil) for Sydling St. Nicholas. The hill lies south-east of the village. Finds are in the Dorchester Museum.

Here at some date between 1300 and 1000 B.C. there developed a complex arrangement of enclosures, tracks and buildings, extending over a distance of 150 yards. One of the enclosures was divided down the middle by a bank. In the western part of this division there stood a circular hut, 27 feet in diameter, with a porched entrance facing south. In the eastern part there are signs of another hut, more oval in shape and a little smaller. To the south of these buildings and in the same enclosure there was a smooth threshing floor and a pond. Around these constructions were small fields and tracks.

Two other sites in Wessex are at Ram's Hill and Stockbridge Down. Ram's Hill, Berkshire, is an oval earth enclosure, 400 feet by 270 feet, with a single entrance facing south. It can be dated to the Middle Bronze Age, but does not appear to have been inhabited, and the assumption is that it was used for animals. The site at Stockbridge Down, Hampshire, consists of a pit, shaped like the figure eight, which had certainly been used as a dwelling-place, for parts of collared urns and of a quern were found there.

At neither of these sites is there anything for the ordinary traveller to investigate today. Some of the surrounding earth banks may date from the Middle Bronze Age, but they are best discussed as features of the Later Bronze Age (see p. 121).

In the south-west the situation is different. Specialized settlements, probably dating from about 1200 B.C., have left their mark on Dartmoor. There the prevailing winds blow from the south and west. In consequence, the eastern side of the moor is the more sheltered and drier. In the Middle Bronze Age this led to the development of two distinct economies within a few miles of one another—pastoralists in the south and west, arable farmers to the east. Both made use of the stone which was everywhere abundant and as a result plenty of evidence has survived concerning the construction of these settlements.

The pastoralists tended to live in groups, each group of huts surrounded by a squat wall about 9 feet thick and 8 feet high made from a core of small stones held in place on both sides by large boulders. Inside this enclosure there might be anything from five to thirty huts scattered about, while square stockpens were built into the side of the settlement wall, or, more occasionally, were free-standing. These villages were sited on south-facing slopes between 1,000 and 1,300 feet above sea-level, conveniently close to running water and to pasture.

The huts themselves were circular, 10 to 25 feet in diameter, their stone walls originally about 4 feet high and 4 feet thick at the base. The doorways faced away from the north and in some of the huts a curved entrance helped to keep the weather out. The roof was tent-shaped, with rafters resting on a central pole and also supported by a ring of poles between centre and circumference, while their lower ends were wedged firmly into the top of the stone walls. Alder was woven into these rafters and the whole topped off with thatch or turf, perhaps held down by stone slabs.

There are variations on this basic plan. The smaller huts, at Grimspound for instance, needed no circle of roof supports; at Dean Moor there is a pair of 'semi-detached' huts; in some huts it is clear that a distinction exists between the lower south slope where the cooking took place, and the upper, drier part which has developed a recess in which to sleep. In the cooking hole in one hut a pot was found in position with a cooking stone still in it.

The most rewarding pastoral settlements to visit are probably those at Dean Moor (SX/660661); at Rider's Rings, South Brent (SX/680645); and at Grimspound (SX/700809). The easiest way to reach Dean Moor is to follow the lane which leads west out of Buckfastleigh to Hayford. The hut circles lie 2 miles beyond. For Rider's Rings, take the lane north out of South Brent to Shipley Bridge. The circles lie 2 miles north up the river Avon. A map is essential for both these groups. Grimspound is much easier, the circles lie to the east of the road that leaves B3212 (Moretonhampstead-Princetown) for Widecombe and quite close to it.

At Grimspound the wall encloses an area of about 4 acres. The enclosure is crossed by a stream at its lower end. The wall is 9 feet thick at the base and was originally about 6 feet high, with an entrance 7 feet wide, nicely paved. There are the foundations of about two dozen huts still visible. The huts vary in diameter from 10 to 15 feet; eight of them have no sign of a hearth and the entrance to these is wider than that of the other huts, it is thought that they may have been used for stock.

The second type of settlement, that of the eastern arable farmers, consisted of six or eight small rectangular fields, usually about a third of an acre in extent, surrounded by a wall of granite slabs and farmed from three or four huts built into the sides of the fields. The huts of these arable settlements are similar in construction to those of the pastoralists already described, but they are significantly larger, with an inside diameter of 20 feet to 40 feet.

Examples of this second type of settlement include Foales Arrishes (SX/737758), Kestor (SX/665867) and Rippon Tor (SX/753759). To reach Foales Arrishes, take the lane east out of Widecombe for 1½ miles. The site is a quarter of a mile south-west of the minor road junction at Hemsworth Gate. There are the remains of eight huts; some of them are badly damaged, but the site is easy to visit, and interesting because there are the remains of long narrow field banks running from the ground to the west between Top Tor and Pill Tor down to the settlement. Finds are in Plymouth Museum. The settlement at Rippon Tor, apparently that of a single family, lies less than a mile from Foales Arrishes to the south of the minor road from Hemsworthy Gate to Haytor Vale.

To reach Kestor, follow the lane west out of Chagford to Teigncombe and Batworthy. The site lies between these two mainly to the south of the road. Finds are in Exeter Museum. There are about twenty-five huts in this settlement. The most interesting is that standing alone in a round enclosure called the Round Pound. It dates from the Iron Age but is, from the traveller's point of view, most conveniently described here. The site is that of a metalworker's hut—the village blacksmith of later times. In one half of this hut was the living area, in the other the working quarters. There was a smelting furnace, still full of iron slag when discovered, a forging pit, a stone anvil, and a pool of water for quenching, from which a covered drain led out under the stone wall of the hut.

Clues to the method of arable cultivation employed at these settlements have been found at a site in another part of the south-west, Gwithian in Cornwall. There investigators discovered variations in the colour of the soil which indicated that the fields were cross-hoed with a hand plough—a bent bough with its tip hardened by burning. There were also spade-marks where cuts had filled up with sand, triangular in shape and 5 inches deep— marks that echo those made by the long-handled spade still in use in parts of Cornwall, Wales and Ireland.

THE LATE BRONZE AGE

It is often difficult accurately to date finds of the Late Bronze Age (around 900 to 500 B.C.). There is a tendency to push material back into the period a little before 900 B.C. or forward into the Iron Age. This is particularly true of the so-called 'Celtic' fields which may turn out to be of any date between 1300 B.C. and Roman times, thus the Dartmoor sites already described range in date from 1200 to 400 B.C. Only detailed knowledge of the individual site can enable the observer to decide where exactly within this long stretch of time any particular 'Celtic' field should be placed. Part of the trouble, of course, is that there was considerable continuity of farming settlements and farming methods during this period. Indeed evidence is steadily accumulating that there are sites, for instance in Devonshire, which have been farmed continuously, even with some continuity of actual field shapes, for the last 3,000 years.

In southern England the earlier part of the age is often referred to by the clumsy title of the Deverel-Rimbury culture. This forbidding name derives from two early type-sites each dating from about 1000 to 900 B.C. Deverel (SY/819990) is the site of a round barrow. It lies between Dorchester and Blandford, on the north side of road A354 about a mile north east of Milborne. It would not be true to say that there is nothing to see there, but what one *does* see is not perhaps what one would expect.

Deverel was excavated in 1824–5 by William Augustus Miles, whose initials can be seen carved on stones at the site. In 1826 Miles allowed his romantic imagination to take charge, describing the scene when

> . . . the blazing pile flinging its lurid beams around, gave notice to the distant tribes of the sad office then performing, while the relentless and officiating priest, plunging his steel into the breast of those unhappy favourites who were doomed to share their master's death, calmly viewed their convulsive agonies; while the mystic song of bards, narrating the exploits of him for whom the fire blazed, the frantic yells and mystic dance of the skin-clad Celts, drowned in an universal clamour, the wild and piercing shrieks of expiring victims; then were the trophies solemnly deposited, then was raised the mound, and then was performed the mystic ceremony of going thrice around the tomb. . . .[1]

It is something of an anti-climax to discover that the excavators built a modern wall round the barrow—still visible. The whole affair exemplifies the strength and the weakness of nineteenth-century archaeology.

About twenty cremations from Late Bronze Age times had been inserted in the barrow—itself of an earlier Middle Bronze Age date. The ashes were contained in a new type of pot—an urn, barrel-shaped, bucket-shaped or globular, 10 to 14 inches in height, rather plain, rather heavy, decorated often with an unimpressive ring of finger-tip decoration about a quarter of the way down the urn. These Deverel urns can be seen in the Bristol City Museum.

Rimbury, the other type-site, lies between road A353 out of Weymouth and Chalbury hill-fort. There is nothing to see. This in itself is typical of the period, for Rimbury is a cemetery, and the Late Bronze Age is a period of flat cemeteries, urn-fields as they are well-called. At Rimbury about 100 cremations were found in separate urns. The urns were used as targets by the first dis-coverers and only nine survived. Eight of these are in the Dor-chester Museum.

---

[1] W. A. Miles, *The Deverel Barrow* (1826), pp. 10–11.

What is known of the Deverel-Rimbury culture? Once again, the new culture is the product of a stimulus from the continent. The urnfield folk arrived from the Franco-Belgian coast, bringing with them plenty of bronze, new industrial and agricultural techniques, and the practice of burying their dead in these urnfields.

This Late Bronze Age is an important one, for it offers the first conclusive evidence of permanent settled farming.

Judging from the bones recovered, the livestock continued to consist of dogs, pigs, sheep and short-horn oxen, and the small horse. The horse had existed in Britain at least from Beaker times, but it was only now that it came to enjoy that position of importance which it held until the second quarter of the twentieth century A.D., when the tractor led to its rapid decline as an element in the working farm life.

One may assume, for the sake of tidiness, that a general pattern of settled agriculture developed in southern England during the 400 or 500 years covered by the general label of 'the Late Bronze Age' though in practice the details vary from area to area. This pattern consisted of small isolated farmsteads, surrounded by a higgledy-piggledy arrangement of little rectangular fields, their economy based to an increasing extent on arable farming, their most valuable instrument a light plough.

On suitable ground stock-farming continued to be the main activity, though it seems to have been now usually combined with static arable areas. For cattle small enclosures were used, varying from a quarter of an acre to about 2 acres in size.

One such enclosure is that at Martin Down Camp, Cranborne Chase (SU/043201). It lies just to the south of road A354 (Salisbury-Blandford), 9 miles out of Salisbury. The camp is typical, 2 acres in size, surrounded by a bank now 2 feet high and a ditch once about 10 feet deep. This ditch was V-shaped. A useful means of identification is the fact that the Late Bronze Age people and their successors normally cut V-shaped ditches, instead of those with a U-shaped profile of the type which had prevailed for 2,000 years. At sites which have been occupied by both earlier and later cultures—for instance, at Hembury Hill (see pp. 32–3) in Devonshire—one can often find examples of both U-shaped and V-shaped profiles in close juxtaposition the one with the other.

The cattle enclosures are very similar to the Neolithic causewayed camps constructed 2,000 years earlier. Similarity of purpose has resulted in similarity of structure. The Late Bronze Age examples have one or more entrances, orientated in any direction, and quite wide, perhaps as much as 90 feet across. The construction of these rather unexciting pounds is brought to life by the fact that at one site a broken bronze spud, the blade of which fitted exactly the still-surviving marks, was found lying in the ditch which it had helped to cut.

In many parts of the chalklands of Wessex a different sort of ditch or earthwork, also constructed in the Late Bronze Age, exists. It takes the form of long linear earthworks. These are seen as boundary ditches, as 'fences' delimiting areas of cattle-ranching, or as barriers to keep cattle out of arable areas. The exact purpose of any particular ditch depends on its siting, and on the relative positions of ditch and bank. When the bank jumps from side to side of the ditch, for instance, its only purpose could have been that of a boundary.

A good place to see these ditches is in the Bourne valley (north-east of Salisbury, road A338 passes through it) where they run at fairly regular intervals down to the river on both sides. The ditches enclose largish areas, perhaps three-quarters of a mile wide and 2 miles in length, and here are assumed to delimit cattle pastures.

The remains of the settlements from which the farmers who constructed these complicated patterns of land-use operated are fragmentary. One must imagine circular timber-framed huts within an enclosed, perhaps stockaded, farmstead—again a picture which recalls the Neolithic settlements.

Evidence for these farmsteads has been found at Boscombe Down East, and Thorny Down (SU/203338), both in Wiltshire.

The site at Thorny Down is probably connected with the ditches described above. It lies on the north side of road A30 (Salisbury-Andover) opposite the road to Winterslow. Here there was a rectangular enclosure delimited by a bank and ditch, enclosing a farmstead covering about half an acre. Within the enclosure was an oblong 'farmhouse', 25 feet by 15 feet, with a porch on one of the long walls. This building was probably divided into two rooms, and was surrounded by eight outbuildings for stock and a number of storage pits, cooking-holes and so on.

Some of the posts at Thorny had rotted and been renewed, clear evidence of continuous, careful maintenance. The remains of saddle-querns were found which had been used for both wheat and barley. Whorls and weights indicated the existence of spinning and of an upright loom. The nearest water was 2 miles away.

This farm seems to have been mainly concerned with stock farming.

In general the floor was clean and the remains that were recovered were found around the postholes where the dust and rubbish had collected when the floor was swept. But there were two disturbing exceptions. On the otherwise bare floor there was a broken bronze bracelet, while outside the house a bronze spearhead lay on the ground. Nothing else. One can construct varying tales of tragedy—or comedy—around this situation, but Thorny Down keeps its secret.

Farmsteads were surrounded by small squarish fields. These, as already noted, remained unchanged in shape throughout Iron Age and Roman times at least until the establishment of Saxon agricultural techniques sometimes as much as 1,500 years later. The dating of any particular field is extraordinarily difficult when, as in Wessex, at least 90 per cent of the fields were still being farmed in Roman times, whatever their date of origin.

The whole tangle of fields and banks, tracks and boundaries represents the successful efforts of men practising a mixed farming economy to adapt their natural surroundings to their artificial needs. The most important single development of this period was the introduction of the light plough. Up till this time the preparation of the ground had been carried out by primitive hoeing with a hand-pick. The new machine was used to break-up the field and then to cross-plough it. An approximately square field was the most convenient shape for its use, so that small rectangular fields now dominated the landscape in many parts of the south.

The new plough not only allowed existing arable areas to be broken up more quickly, more easily and more efficiently, it also led to the extension of arable farming to slightly more 'difficult' areas. Better farming, more extensive farming, meant more food and this, in turn, undoubtedly led to a rise in population, at least in southern England.

The Late Bronze Age was *the* age of Bronze. The metal, which had been available in relatively small—though growing—quantities for hundreds of years, now became comparatively plentiful. New methods of working and new products made their appearance. The most advanced groups seem to have had about ten times as many metal objects as any earlier British culture had possessed. Socketed axe-heads, socketed spearheads, swords that could thrust or slash as required, saws, knives, gouges, chisels, the tools of the carpenter and the metal smith—all were brought to perfection by the Late Bronze Age immigrants. The new techniques of metal-working consisted of beating, riveting and soldering, instead of relying solely on casting.

The tide of change was not all one way. There was an exchange of methods and patterns of work between, at the one extreme, Ireland, and, at the other, European communities extending from Spain to Scandinavia. The highland zone as usual lagged behind in these developments; to take a late example, it does not appear that a local bronze industry developed in Wales before 750 B.C. However, the time-gap was at least becoming narrower.

Bronze products were brought to the remoter areas by itinerant metalworkers—'tinkers' is not a term carrying sufficient prestige for the importance of these lonely craftsmen. At Sumburgh Head, in the Shetland Islands of the far north, the local settlement—only three or four houses—was in the sixth century B.C. still enduring a Neolithic existence similar in many ways to that of Skara Brae, 1,000 years earlier (see pp. 57–8). There had, it is true, been some developments: a few cattle were now kept and the floor of the cow pen was dished in order to make easier the collection of dung, the earliest example of this particular improvement yet known in the British Isles. This isolated, lonely group were not backward, in the normally accepted sense of the word. A sign of imaginative adaptation was their use of the vertebra of a stranded whale as a ring to which the cattle could be tethered.

At this late date a metalsmith, perhaps from Ireland, certainly skilled in Irish methods, arrived at Sumburgh and set up shop. He established a smithy and a foundry and turned out axes and swords, pins and knives.

His arrival meant that suddenly the settlement at Sumburgh Head had leapt 1,000 years into the Bronze Age. The effect can be imagined. There was soon even a little iron slag at this Shetland settlement. The ripples of progress were spreading through the British Isles with increasing speed.

In Wessex, at Donhead St. Mary, a metalsmith's hoard contained eleven axes, the mould for making axe-heads, a drill, a hammer, hanks of wire, unworked metal, and a whetstone—all the moveable equipment required. At Wick in north-west Somerset, a similar hoard contained 147 bits and pieces. These included copper ingots, and almost sixty pieces of broken or damaged bronze implements which could be melted down again, metal left in the funnel when a mould was being filled, and the finished product—axe-heads, knives, gouges.

Another hoard, this time from Guilsford, Montgomeryshire, is interesting on two counts. It includes a mis-cast spearhead; the core had not been put in when casting, and so it had no socket to fit onto the spear shaft. The hoard also contained examples of both the older Irish palstave and the later English socketed axe—both clearly in demand at the same date, the end of the eighth century B.C., in this cultural borderland.

Plenty of other hoards have been found, especially in Wales and Scotland. In general these metal-workers' hoards were almost certainly buried in times of danger and never recovered. Each represents a personal tragedy in an impersonal age.

In the improvement of individual tools and weapons the high-land zone seems to have produced one original type. A circular shield was developed, about 3 feet in diameter—a pattern that survived in the Highlands until the time of the Jacobite rebellions in the eighteenth century A.D. These shields were made of wood, of riveted metal, or of leather pressed while wet into a wooden mould and left to harden. All included a strengthening central boss above the hand-grip.

On the other hand, the slashing, leaf-shaped sword, with its long hilt, was a continental invention which slowly replaced the rapier during this period.

A typical product of the Late Bronze Age, not available in earlier times, were the great cauldrons made of sheets of riveted bronze and equipped with rings that could be used as handles, or through which hooks could be used to suspend them over the fire. These were not a western invention, but seem to have orgin-ated in the eastern Mediterranean world. They figure largely in Homer, while in the west they are potent symbols in the Celtic myths of the highland zone, myths that were still being composed and recited 1,000 years later in the sixth century A.D.—symbols of power, of hospitality, of birth and rebirth. At a more prosaic level, two cauldrons from a sacrificial hoard found at Llyn Fawr in South Wales show marks of rubbing on the rims and handles, which indicate quite clearly that they were stored upside down when not in use, a shaft of light through the darkness on Bronze Age household management. These cauldrons are in the National Museum of Wales, Cardiff.

With this emphasis on metal, the button or toggle passed out of favour for about 500 years, its place taken by a long and often ornamental safety-pin. What has been termed 'the waistcoat age' was, for the time being, over.

Not all the hoards recovered from this period are of bronze. Important caches of gold have also been found. At Towednack, Lelant, Cornwall, two twisted torcs, four bracelets—two of them unfinished—and three coiled ingots were discovered. These are now in the British Museum. The torcs—twisted collars or armlets —were made by beating the gold bars into a triangular cross-section, hammering out the angles so formed into dished flanges, twisting the resulting shape clockwise, and then gently turning the finished product into a circle or spiral—a sophisticated series of operations, requiring the ability to visualize a finished form that lay several stages ahead. The final diameter of the torc was normally almost 4 or 5 inches and in the Towednack hoard the larger of these complicated ornaments was nearly 4 feet in length.

The greatly increased trade in metal ore and metal products followed the old routes, the seaways of the Channel, the North Sea and the Irish Sea, the land tracks pioneered in Neolithic times, and the older chalk and limestone ways. By their nature even the land routes have left little trace of their existence and they are difficult to date. Sometimes a Roman road crosses a track. Clearly the track is older than the road—but how much older?

The easiest to follow today are those of the chalk and limestone ridges, tracks which have probably been in use continuously since the ice sheet receded, so that to walk along one is to experience the whole of prehistory. It is a pleasant way of doing so, the going is easy, the views extensive, the turf encouraging; Stukeley said that he found the Wansdyke downs "softer to walk upon than a Turkey carpet".

These trackways start—or finish—in Wessex and a detailed description of some of the best sections can be found in L. V. Grinsell, *The Archaeology of Wessex*, pages 296–301.

Probably the best-known, and certainly the longest, of these early tracks is the Icknield Way. The Way starts near Swindon and follows the north slope of the Berkshire Downs. It crosses the Thames at the Goring Gap above Reading and then picks up the north slope of the Chilterns, which it continues to follow after they have changed their name to the East Anglian Heights, coming to an end in Norfolk after covering a distance of about 150 miles. It is not really practicable to follow its whole course on foot, if only because along its eastern length modern roads often overlie it, but with a car one can drive parallel to the Way, stopping at intervals to sample the track and the prehistoric sites that lie along it.

A good stretch of a different track, one that is easily reached and has the additional advantage of taking in three important sites, is the Berkshire Ridgway that runs along the Downs east from Swindon to the Thames at Goring, a distance of about 25 miles. It passes Wayland's Smithy and the Iron Age sites of Uffington Castle, Uffington White Horse, Alfred's Castle and Segsbury Castle. The Ridgway is on the crest of the Downs, the Icknield Way on the slope, above the spring-line but below the crest. There is very little doubt that the Ridgway is the older. Once both tracks had come into use the lower Icknield Way was probably used in summer, while in very wet weather or in winter, traders took the higher and drier Ridgway.

Towards the close of the Late Bronze Age a specialized form of artificial timber trackway developed, sections of which, precisely because of the special nature of the situation, have survived.

They are found in Somerset where there is an area of marsh and fen—still liable today to flood in winter—which includes a good deal of peat. Late Bronze Age articles have for some time been found in this peat, indicating the settlement of the scattered 'islands' of higher ground. More recently it has become clear that these were connected with the 'mainland', the Polden Hills, and sometimes with one another, by trackways of timber. Sections of several of these tracks have been discovered, the marshy conditions having preserved the wood. There is nothing to see on the spot—though the scenery is exciting in its own peculiar way—but finds and photographs are in the museums at Glastonbury and Taunton. The tracks are similar in some ways to the three dating from Secondary Neolithic times (see p. 38).

One of the Bronze Age trackways has been identified over a distance of $1\frac{1}{2}$ miles. The foundation was of brushwood and on this were laid heavy pieces of oak and birch. There was a wooden kerb and the whole construction was held in place by vertical timbers together with mortise and tenon jointing. These trackways seem to have been constructed at varying dates between 900 and 450 B.C., and they probably reflect the difficulties encountered by the local inhabitants as the area became increasingly marshy.

For the comparatively settled conditions of the Late Bronze Age were coming to an end. Two radical changes occurred. One was a deterioration in the climate. The warm and dry Sub-Boreal climate which had lasted unchanged for so long gave place about 600 B.C. or a little earlier to colder and wetter conditions (Sub-Atlantic). Throughout Britain life became much harder; the track-

ways of the Somerset Levels were drowned, and everywhere settlements had to be stouter, more weather-proof—a bonus for the
archaeologist.

The second change was the arrival of new men, using iron.

VIII

THE IRON AGE:

500 B.C. to A.D. 50

1. PEACE AND COMMERCE

Some time in the early fifth century B.C., perhaps about 475 B.C.
individual groups of people, sailing from the Low Countries and
the northern coast of France, began to make landings at various
points along the south and east coasts of Britain. In the south
they appear to have occupied the natural harbours of Lulworth
and Hengistbury Head, for at these places they threw up fortifications (Bindon Hill and Double Dykes) in which the ditches are on
the landward side and clearly designed to protect the beach-head
against attacks from the interior.

It was not in any way a concerted invasion, the settlers came
from widely separated areas on the mainland of Europe, but they
shared one common characteristic—they were all representatives
of the Celtic Iron Age culture.

Iron, unlike the copper and tin that were required to make
bronze, is relatively abundant and widespread. In consequence
the new culture with its accompanying economic prosperity and
superior weapons of war, was more general than the Bronze Age
culture had ever been. Moreover the ripples of civilization spread
more rapidly from one centre to another than they had done
1,000 years earlier. Large parts of Europe shared a common way
of life to a greater extent than had been true in the past, at least
outside the Mediterranean area.

The Celtic culture was a self-supporting economy, based on
iron, crops and herds, ruled by a warrior aristocracy, astounding
its southern neighbours by the quantities of beer drunk and meat

eaten—especially boiled pork—and producing poor buildings but great art.

In northern Europe the Iron Age had centred first, about 650 B.C., on Hallstatt in West Germany. Two hundred years later a more sophisticated culture, known as the La Tène from a site in Switzerland, developed. At some time between these two dates, and certainly by 500 B.C., a dribble of iron objects began to reach Britain.

It could be argued that the Iron Age really marks the end of our prehistory, for it is at this point in time that there occurs the first written evidence for the existence of these islands.

About the year 550 B.C. there is documentary information that the inhabitants of Brittany were trading with Ireland ('Ierne'— Eire) and England ('Albion'). At last we know what other people called us. The more familiar names arrived a little later, but still well within the confines of the period. About 330–325 B.C. a Greek merchant, Pytheas of Marseilles, wrote of the 'Pretanic Islands', a name which in the Roman world became 'Britannia'.

The Iron Age in Britain has been sub-divided by archaeologists into three periods: Iron Age A, beginning about 450 B.C. and derived from the Hallstatt culture; Iron Age B, dating from the third century B.C., the La Tène culture; and Iron Age C, represented by Breton and Belgic invaders, refugees from the continent at various dates after 120 B.C. All shared, however, many common characteristics and what follows is a generalized description of the Celtic culture, derived partly from classical descriptions of life in Gaul.

The Iron Age peoples in Britain were more important than any groups so far described. They overran the natives, drowned their differences, and eventually came to form the bulk of the populations, at least in southern Britain (matters were rather different north of the Cheviots), a position of importance which they maintained in a fashion even during the Roman occupation. For in the south Celtic society does not seem to have been finally destroyed until the Saxon invasions 1,000 years after the first Iron Age settlers had reached these shores. So, if you have a British prehistoric ancestor, it is most likely, statistically, that he was one of these Iron Age immigrants.

What did they look like, these possible ancestors of ours? Fortunately, they were great artists; fortunately, too, they were in close contact with classical sculptors and writers. By taking the lowest common denominator, as it were, of all the available sculptures and descriptions one can construct a generalized picture for the family album.

As a race they were tall, with a fair skin, blue eyes and blond hair. The men wore flowing moustaches—but no beard—and grew their hair long, keeping it swept back and smeared into place by a thick wash of lime.

A classical statue which matches the written descriptions is that known as the 'Dying Gaul'. The copy of the Greek original is in Rome. In Britain the most evocative piece of sculpture is the native head found at Bath and now in the museum there. The Bath head presumably represents the god of the hot springs, and its creator has developed the flowing hair and moustaches of the Celt so that they grew almost imperceptibly into the magical waters welling up and flowing out from their divine protector and progenitor.

Combine the noble savage of the Roman artist and the rough god of the Celtic carver and one probably has a fairly accurate picture of a Celtic man.

The Celts were the first Britons to wear trousers. This useful, inelegant garment was developed in northern continental Europe, a necessity for horsemen in cold climates. Early in their migrations the Celts adopted trousers, cut tight at the ankle, from the inhabitants of the sub-arctic areas of northern Europe and Asia.

Trousers were associated in the classical mind with barbarians and as such were the object of amused or contemptuous comment —Greeks and Romans regarded them as highly peculiar, rather as southerners today regard the kilt. The Romans were shocked when their emperor Augustus adopted in old age the practice of wearing woollen pants, though they accepted this aberration because of his immense prestige. Augustus had become a Churchillian figure who might be allowed his eccentricities.

On the upper part of the body the Celts wore a loose tunic, belted and sleeved. This in turn could be covered by a cloak or blanket, woven in stripes or checks of bright colours, fringed at the ends and fastened on one shoulder with a large brooch. This was a general-purpose garment, still in use in sixteenth-century Ireland, when great parts of the country were living in a state of civilization not very different from that of the Iron Age—a fact which helps to explain the atrocities committed there by the Elizabethan English. One of these Elizabethans, the poet, Edmund Spenser, described the Irish cloak as "a fit house for an outlaw, a meet bed for a rebel, and an apt cloak for a thief".

The classical reaction to the general appearance of the Celts was expressed by Diodorus Siculus in the second century B.C. when he wrote that the Celts "let their moustaches grow so long that their mouths are covered up; and so when they eat, they get entangled in the food, while their drink is taken in, as it were, through a strainer", adding that they wore "amazing clothes, shirts with patterns and dyed all kinds of colours, and trousers called *brakai*". The cloth was woven from wool or from the fibres of flax and nettles. At Harlyn Bay, Cornwall, the discovery of *Purpura lapillus* shells provides evidence for the source of a purple dye, but most colours were vegetable-derived.

The free men wore jewellery. A heavy brooch fastened the cloak. It operated on the principle of the safety-pin—that simple object which had made its first appearance in Bronze Age times and that has survived, unimproved because unimprovable, to the present day. Celtic men also wore a metal neck-ring, open at the front and known to archaeologists as a torc—though twisted examples are comparatively rare in Britain.

Classical writers agree in their descriptions of the Celtic temperament. They saw the Celts as lively, quick-tempered, fond of warfare, but with a certain degree of natural good manners—considering that they were barbarians. Strabo, a typical commentator, wrote of those in Gaul, "The whole nation is war-mad, high-spirited and quick to fight, though in other ways simple and not uncouth."

Spenser found matters unchanged almost 2,000 years later, observing in his *View of the Present State of Ireland* that the inhabitants were "a nation ever acquainted with wars" who in their "fury tread down and trample underfoot all, both human and divine, things".

The Celtic social structure was firmly based on the individual farm but, like the Bronze Age society which it replaced, it was dominated by a warrior aristocracy and organized in a close-knit tribal system.

Strabo speaks of a 'nation', but the Celts were not a nation in any political sense, either in Gaul or in Britain. Quite small areas were organized as a 'people', under a 'king'. These units may be regarded as clans. The royal family held the land in trust for the clan, and descent was not necessarily by primogeniture.

In southern England five independent statelets established themselves: the Dumnonii in Cornwall and Devon; the Dobunni in the Cotswold area, the Durotriges in Dorset the Atrebates in

Hampshire, and the Trinovantes in Essex. Later the picture was complicated by other arrivals.

Beneath the king was a class of nobles (which included the druids), and below these came the free men, organized in family groups sharing a common great-grandfather ('kins'). At the base of the pyramid there were, as usual, the unfree. Caesar observed the distinction in Gaul in the first century B.C., writing of "the common people who are treated almost like slaves" and of "the privileged classes . . . Knights and Druids".

Once again Elizabethans were making much the same observations about Ireland, Sir Henry Sidney writing: "There are two sorts of people in Ireland to be considered of: the one called the Kerne, the other the Churls. The Kerne bred up in idleness and naturally inclined to mischief and wickedness, the Churl willing to labour and take pains, if he might peaceably enjoy the fruits thereof". By that time the Druids had gone, but their spiritual descendants, the bards, survived, exercising so strong an influence that their activities were prohibited by English law. Perhaps the old religion also survived for, on the old Celtic festivals, the eve of May Day and Midsummer Eve, the English marvelled at the celebrations: "what watching, what rattling, what tinkling upon pans and candlesticks, what strewing of herbs, what clamours".

Within this emotional and social framework the Celts lived by a mixture of pastoral and arable farming. They developed and adapted the Late Bronze Age methods and patterns of cultivation. There was perhaps rather more emphasis on corn-growing and rather less on sheep-farming. In the south there was a rapid expansion of downland settlement, almost to saturation point, but north of the Icknield Way life was still predominantly pastoral. Caesar commented that near the coast the population was large and the landscape peppered with farms, while the tribes of the interior did not for the most part grow corn, but lived on meat and milk.

The main crop was still barley, but wheat had regained a little of its old importance. Two varieties of the latter were now grown, the long-established emmer, and the new spelt, the spikes of which could not be threshed until they had been gently baked to make them brittle. Oats and rye were newcomers; 1,500 years later these last had become the staple corn crops of the medieval peasant.

By Iron Age times a light plough drawn by two oxen had already come into use. The new instrument had been developed in the

Mediterranean area and on the light soil with which it could cope. The landscape was over-ruled with a pattern of Celtic fields of a shape suitable for cross-ploughing. Towards the close of the Iron Age Belgic invaders introduced a heavier plough and cultivation of more difficult soils began to take place.

These fields, rarely larger than about 400 feet by 260 feet, were surrounded by earthen banks and evidence suggests that within them the final furrows were about 15 inches apart. South-facing hill-slopes were cultivated, as well as more level ground, and on these slopes the lower edge of the field was supported by an artificial terrace, or by a natural bank formed as the soil moved downhill and piled up against the field boundary during ploughing. Under the right lighting conditions—that is, when the shadows are reasonably long—these banks (lynchets) stand out. There is still controversy concerning the age of individual examples. Some are probably earlier than the Iron Age, many are certainly later, but perhaps the majority date from this period.

This Celtic field system from its first appearance in the Late Bronze Age to its general disappearance in Saxon times was in existence far longer than any other English field-pattern—longer than the better-known medieval strips, and much longer than the modern pattern of hedged fields which replaced those strips and which is now in its turn beginning to vanish.

When the grain grown in these fields had been harvested by means of flint or iron sickles, it was threshed, the ears of spelt having first been heated to loosen the grain. The corn was then divided into two heaps. The lesser of these, about a third of the crop, was stored in small rectangular granaries, rendered rat-proof by being raised on posts, and kept for use as seed-corn in the next season. The remainder, the food-corn, was put in storage pits about 5 feet wide and 5 feet deep, wider at the bottom than the top and often lined with basket-work. It has been estimated that a good-sized pit of this type could have held a ton of corn, the product of about 4 acres of arable land.

The pits soon became infected with mould. When this happened fresh ones were dug and the old ones filled in. Numerous pits of this type are a feature of Iron Age settlement sites; on the older maps they are often described, incorrectly, as 'pit-dwellings'. (On the chalk down pits were also sometimes dug for marling, and then filled with rubbish.) In the areas occupied by the Belgae towards the close of the Iron Age the food-corn was usually stored in jars rather than in pits.

Before the food-corn could be stored it was dried in ovens made of cob, with domed roofs and clay floors. The drying process was carried out by the use of heated flints or other stones and these fire-marked fragments can often still be found in the storage area.

The corn was milled as required, a rotary quern eventually replacing the older saddle-shaped quern.

The Somerset lake villages have provided examples of the end-product of all this agricultural activity in the form of the still-identifiable remains of bread and buns!

The stock kept included the short-horn ox, the horned sheep, goats, pigs, ponies and a variety of breeds of dog—much the same range as that of the Late Bronze Age. The cattle were perhaps rather similar to the present-day herd of wild cattle at Chillingham in Northumberland. Chillingham lies to the east of road A697 (Newcastle-Wooler).

The high proportion of bones found to have belonged to young animals indicates that a good deal of the stock was slaughtered each year, presumably in the autumn to provide reserves of food for the winter and to reduce the problem of wintering the animals. There is evidence from classical writers that cattle-raiding was considered an honourable occupation—an attitude that remained true of the highland zone of Britain until at least the sixteenth century. The more settled areas, of course, took a rather different view, as indicated by the English nursery rhyme which blackguards the Welsh

> Taffy was a Welshman, Taffy was a thief,
> Taffy came to my house and stole a side of beef,
> I went to Taffy's house, Taffy was not home,
> Taffy came to my house and stole a marrow-bone.

The sites of a number of Iron Age settlements are known—in contrast with the paucity of information for the Bronze Age—and a general pattern is observable. A typical settlement consisted of a round house within a stockade, separated from its neighbours by perhaps 4 acres of fields and an area of downland pasture, with a stockpen, storage pits and cob ovens inside the enclosure.

The best-understood individual site is probably that of Little Woodbury, one and a half miles south of Salisbury. (There is nothing to be seen on the spot.) Little Woodbury seems to have been occupied for about 300 years and to have controlled perhaps

15 acres of land, though not more than half of this would have been farmed at any one time.

It was clearly an important farm, for the stockade enclosed an area about 400 feet in width. There was only one building, but that was exceptionally large, a circular timber-built structure 45 feet in diameter, with an inner ring of posts to support the rafters and four large tree-trunks set at the corners of a central square within which lay the hearth. There was no chimney, the smoke went out through a hole in the roof or swirled around inside if there was no draught.

Little Woodbury is so large that it must have housed not only the owner and his family but also his servants, all living and sleeping together in the one enclosure as in the rectangular Saxon halls of a later time. The area between the outer wall and the inner ring of posts may have been divided into separate 'rooms' for humans or stalls for animals.

The house had a porched entrance and a drain led from the hearth to this entrance. Outside in the surrounding enclosure there had been dug at various times at least 360 food and rubbish pits. During the war scare about 250 B.C. (see p.149) some alterations were made to the basic plan, including the digging of a defensive ditch.

A very different type of settlement developed in the marshy Somerset Levels at Meare and Glastonbury. The peculiar conditions allowed an unprecedented amount of material to survive, but the very fact that the conditions were unusual meant that the settlements were themselves of a specialized type.

There were three settlements, one at Glastonbury and two at Meare. The Glastonbury Lake Village (ST/493408) lies 1½ miles out of the town. Take B3151 towards Meare and then follow the first lane to the right. In the field one can just see a number of barely-raised grass-covered platforms, the remains of about ninety huts packed onto a 2-acre site. Four or 5 miles north west of Glastonbury were the East and West Meare Lake Villages (ST/445422), each consisting of about sixty huts. Finds from the three villages are in the museums at Glastonbury and Taunton.

It is believed that the settlements were founded by Dumnonian colonists who arrived by way of the Bristol Channel about 150 B.C. They are seen as a group of artist-craftsmen, farming the 'mainland' of the Mendips for their food, but primarily engaged in trade. They had trading contacts with Cornwall, Dorset and the Forest of Dean, and examples of a Meare speciality, clear glass beads with a yellow glass thread in them, have been found as far away as Ireland. Later, Venetic refugees fleeing from Julius Caesar's campaign in Brittany joined the settlements. Later still, the inhabitants appear to have been massacred by members of the last Iron Age invasion group, the Belgae.

The villages differ slightly in detail, but share a common pattern. The sites were determined by patches of ground slightly higher and firmer than the surrounding marsh. The Glastonbury village was protected by a stockade in addition to its natural defences. The huts themselves were circular, having a diameter of 18 to 28 feet, their walls of wattle and daub, their roofs thatched. The platform on which each hut stood was really a little artificial island (crannog) made of logs, brushwood and clay. These floors, and in particular the hearths, had to be rebuilt in successive layers as they gradually sank into the soft ground below. In addition to these general features, Glastonbury possessed a jetty or landing-stage.

Lake village pottery was decorated with particularly attractive patterns composed of scroll-shapes and circles, scratched into the clay in a flowing pattern of lines and cross-hatching. Bronze-working was practised and a fine bowl of hammered sheets of bronze held together with rivets has survived more or less intact. The remains of upright looms have been found, together with spindle-whorls, loom weights and weaving combs—these last usually made of red deer antler.

Not surprisingly, fishing was a major activity and quantities of metal sinkers have been recovered. The lead for these came from the deposits on the Mendip 'mainland' 9 or 10 miles to the north, but the crude metal was probably worked up in the village, for triangular clay crucibles with a spout at each corner have been found, one with traces of metal—in this case copper—still in it. Wooden tubs and bowls indicate the presence of craftsmen-carpenters, using the recently-introduced pole-lathe for turning the wood.

Products of the fields and pasture of the 'mainland' found in the villages include carbonized grains of emmer wheat and barley, and the remains of cattle, sheep, pigs and goats.

As far as the more luxurious side of life is concerned, there have been considerable finds of bronze rings and jewellery of La Tène design, together with armlets of Kimmeridge shale. Dice have been recovered, and a handful of coins dating from the later years of the settlements.

Much of this was almost certainly not special to the Glastonbury area. It is just that here have survived the objects which have perished in other areas, the household and industrial impedimenta of everyday Iron Age life.

It is time that something was said about the metal which gave the age its name. The technique required for iron-working was entirely different from that which had been developed by the bronzesmiths. Workers in bronze melted their metals at a fairly low temperature and then cast the finished object in a mould. Iron, on the other hand, has a much higher melting-point than tin or copper. Moreover, cast iron is an unsatisfactory product, for it breaks very easily.

About 1400 B.C. the difficulties were first overcome in Asia Minor and from that centre the knowledge of iron-working spread slowly outwards until it finally reached Britain, about 1,000 years later.

The method of working was as follows. Crude iron ore was mixed with charcoal and heated in a bellows-blown fire, until a temperature was reached at which the mixture formed a spongy malleable lump, or 'bloom' as it was later called. The bloom was hammered until the cinders and impurities had been driven out. The resulting 'wrought' iron could then be reheated and beaten into the required shape in a blacksmith's forge. The iron weapons and utensils produced were harder and sharper than those made of bronze, though they rusted much more easily.

In Britain iron was worked in several areas, of which the Forest of Dean to the west of the Severn estuary was perhaps the first. Sussex, the great iron-working centre of medieval and early modern times, does not seem to have been developed before the first century B.C.

Bars of wrought iron became a medium of exchange, a form of currency. 'Sets' of bars exist in the ascending order of weight: 1, 2, 4, 6, 8, 16—which provides a clue to the mathematical pattern of thought of their makers.

The other minerals mined were copper, lead and tin. A valuable by-product of lead-mining was silver. Copper continued to be required as the main constituent in bronze, and there is evidence that Cornish tin was an important export.

As early as the sixth century there had certainly been trading contacts between Cornwall, Brittany and southern Spain. It was probably the conquest of this last area by the Carthaginians and the consequent economic disruption of links with Greek settlements in the western Mediterranean such as Marseilles ('Massilia') that prompted direct voyages from these colonies to Brittany and Cornwall. Hints of one such voyage have survived in the form of references by later writers to the account given by Pytheas of Marseilles, the Greek merchant already mentioned, who sailed to Britain about the years 330 to 325 B.C.

In the second century Diodorus Siculus describes how "the inhabitants of that part of Britain . . . prepare the tin, working very carefully the earth in which it is produced. The ground is rocky, but it contains earthy veins, the produce of which is ground down, smelted, and purified." He goes on to say that the purified metal was then hammered into an ingot shaped like an astragalus, the upper bone in the foot, and an ingot of exactly this shape has been recovered from the Fal estuary. It is 2 feet 10 inches in length, weighs nearly 160 pounds, and can be seen in Truro Museum— ocular proof that Diodorus was not repeating legends, but reporting the exact truth.

The ingots were then, he continues, taken to "a certain island lying off Britain called *Ictis*", where "during the ebb-tide the intervening space is left dry, and they carry over the tin in abundance in their wagons"—a description which fits St. Michael's Mount in Cornwall. (There is also evidence of an Iron Age trading settlement at Mount Batten, Plymouth, but no proof that this one was necessarily involved in the tin trade.)

Diodorus goes on to describe the route by which Cornish tin reached the Mediterranean. Gallic merchants took it across the Channel, a voyage that might take as long as four days. From Brittany it was moved overland to the mouth of the Loire and then shipped coastwise south to the estuary of the Garonne. From there it was taken across southern France by way of the Carcassonne gap to the lower Rhone valley and the Greek colony at Marseilles.

In view of the distance and the nature of the route taken it is not surprising that there is no evidence of direct contact between the tin men and the Mediterranean area, but Greek objects— cups, jugs, coins and so on—have been found in Cornwall. Coins struck after 326 B.C. by Alexander III of Macedon and of 93–2 B.C. issued by a Roman official in Macedonia were found at Holne in Devonshire and can be seen in the Torquay Museum.

In spite of the fact that the peninsula was the source of a much-desired product, there are no signs that the area was particularly rich. There was no great flowering of culture as there had been in earlier times in Wessex when that part of England profited by its position on a trade route. The reasons are not difficult to discover. Tin production was in the hands of small groups of working tinners. There was no wealthy noble class. The tinners were primary producers and their trade was at the mercy of foreign merchants, more wily and in a much stronger economic position than the tinners themselves.

Seen from the other end of the trade route, matters appeared in a different light. Diodorus wrote that the tinners were "very fond of strangers" and that contact with merchants had "civilized their manner of life". He might be a Victorian trader writing of African natives.

Bronze-working and flint-knapping continued. Other crafts for which there is evidence in the Iron Age include the working of Kimmeridge shale, and the production of salt by pouring sea-water over heated stones, a method employed in Dorset and in Lincolnshire.

A great amount of the pottery in use was much the same as in the closing stages of the Bronze Age, coarse coiled pots with little or no decoration on them. The use of the potter's wheel, however, led to the appearance of much smoother forms and, probably for the same reason, a finer type of clay was used. New shapes were produced, including a large jar decorated with chevrons filled with chalk and—more unusual and more easily recognizable—small angular bowls covered with iron oxide (haematite) and polished so that they acquired a metallic finish resembling that of bronze. These were often highly decorated. In La Tène times the decoration on most forms of pottery consisted of flowing geometrical patterns, characteristic and beautiful.

Caesar listed the exports from Britain as consisting of slaves; lead, tin and silver; grain; a certain number of animals for food, and hunting dogs.

Imports consisted of luxuries such as wine and oil, Greek pottery and classical bronze-work. Britain also received from the continent two very different gifts—from the classical world, coinage, and from the Celtic world a highly developed form of abstract art, that of the La Tène culture.

It was in the last stages of the Iron Age that classical coins in comparatively large numbers reached Britain. The great coin of the ancient world, surpassing anything produced by the Romans, was the gold stater of Philip II of Macedon, minted about 350 B.C. The history of the dispersion of this coin throws light on several aspects of the period, including the attitude of mind of Iron Age artists.

Large numbers of staters passed into circulation in the Roman republic after the defeat of Macedon in 167 B.C. Soon Rome was copying the design and—as usual in Roman affairs—the copy was an accurate but lifeless imitation of the brilliant orginal. Before long the Gallic tribes were imitating the Roman imitations. Their copies were inaccurate, but full of life—though not the life of the Macedonian orginals. Finally, about 75 B.C., these Gallic coins reached Britain—where they in turn were imitated. In the south east at the very close of the pre-Christian era, the British began to inscribe their coins. Writing—of a sort—had arrived.

The coins are no longer of gold, but of an alloy of gold, silver and copper. The Durotriges of Dorset had a mint, if that is not too grand a term, at their fort on Hengistbury Head, and while they received the design for their coins from their neighbours to the east, the silver was imported from the south-west, from Callington in Cornwall.

To the east, in Hampshire, Eppillus of the Atrebates, was the first chieftain to use the title king on his coins; the full inscription reads: "*Epp* [Eppillus] *Rex* [King] *Calle* [Calleva Atrebatum =Silchester]". These developments did not have time to spread farther before the Roman conquest. The kingdom of the Dumnones in the south-west never struck a coinage of its own, nor did the chieftains of the north and west.

The use of inscriptions is remarkable; the designs on these coins are even more so. These bits of metal the size of one's thumb nail—the copies of copies of copies—contain all the elements of the Macedonian orginals, but re-arranged. The horses' legs are there, as are the wheels of the chariot and so on, but all disposed in a pattern of dots and dashes and curlicues as beautiful as the original coin, but representing a completely different artistic tradition.

From the earliest times Celtic art had tended to be abstract in approach, geometric in composition. This tendency was reinforced and purified in areas exposed to La Tène influence. As far as Britain is concerned the greatest age of Celtic Art is the century that lies between the years 50 B.C. and A.D. 50 The art contrasts plain areas with patterned ones. The contrast may be between smooth surface and repoussé, plain metal and cross-hatching, self-colour and bright enamel.

Of these decorative devices the most refined is the technique of the La Tène champlevé. In champlevé the pattern is first outlined on the object when it is cast, a low socket being made on the surface along the bounding lines of the pattern. The areas delimited by these sockets are then filled with enamel of the appropriate colour—red or blue—and this is fused into place. The final effect is that the surface of the enamel lies on a level with that of the surrounding metal.

Abstract art is, by definition, not easily described in words. This is an art of arcs and curves and circles, never of straight lines and right angles. For this reason, there is always a hint of natural forms behind the abstraction. Stare long enough, one feels, and the patterns, balanced but asymmetrical, will give up their secret, will resolve themselves into faces, into foliage.

The best way to understand this art is to look at it, the best place to do so is in the British Museum. Consider the lovely bronze mirror back found at St. Keverne, Cornwall, the scabbard mount from Witham, the bronze shield from the Thames, the bronze masks from Stanwick in Yorkshire.

In Ireland this patterning survived for hundreds of years, finding expression for instance in the illuminated letters of the Book of Kells, executed in the seventh century A.D. and now in Trinity College, Dublin.

The most dramatic—and certainly the largest—example of Iron Age art in Britain is the White Horse at Uffington (SU/302867) in Berkshire. To reach it, take B4507 (Swindon-Wantage) and turn south at the appropriate sign. Southern England is full of white horses carved on hillsides, but Uffington is the only one that dates from prehistoric times.

Three hundred and sixty-five feet long, the horse was probably cut about 50 B.C. It is very similar in design to that on the coins of the Atrebates who occupied the area to the south, and to the bronze horse from their capital, Silchester, now in the British Museum. Perhaps it was a tribal badge. Its most remarkable features are the elegant stylisation, the accuracy with which it has been laid out—stand on the spot and one can see nothing, somehow or other the pattern must have been created by observers viewing the area from a distance—and the fact that it has survived, apparently little changed, for about 2,000 years.

The survival of the White Horse is due to the fact that the outline has been periodically cleared of weeds and encroaching vegetation. Recordings of these 'scourings' exist from 1650 onwards and the obligation to scour was included in many title-deeds in the area. The cleaning was accompanied by festivities but, perhaps surprisingly, it does not appear to have been attached to any particular day of the year. This may be explained by the fact that it was a political and not a religious emblem. There is an accurate description of the scouring of 1857 in *Tom Brown's Schooldays*. Nowadays the work is carried out by a government department.

2.   RELIGION, WARFARE AND CONQUEST

A little is known of the Celtic religion, but information concerning the individual Celtic gods and goddesses is scarce, particularly in Britain, and votive statues are likely to be unidentifiable. The main personages were apparently Dagda, the all-competent male god; Maeve, the mare-queen; and the triple goddess.

A number of stone figures of doubtful identity survive. Many made of wood must have perished. In the nineteenth century a wooden figure in oak, about 13·3 inches high, was found in clay workings at Teigngrace in the lower Teign valley. Holes indicate that it once had moveable arms and opinion is divided as to whether it was a toy or a god. The best places to see stone gods and goddesses are in Eire.

Certainly there were, on occasion, human sacrifices. Many classical writers speak with prim disapproval of this 'barbarous' practice. Not all sacrifices were human, though. Votive offerings were the normal procedure, and in this connection a remarkable and unique discovery was made in 1943 at Llyn Cerrig Bach in Anglesey. In that year a mechanical digger employed to build an airfield began to bring up from the edge of the lake a miscellaneous collection of objects. About 140 of these are now in the National Museum of Wales in Cardiff. They include the bones of animals, weapons, part of a trumpet, iron currency bars, pieces of chariots, steel tyres from something between ten and twenty of these vehicles, two cauldrons, wooden spear-shafts, bronze plaques, iron chains and so on. The objects date from about 200 B.C. to A.D. 60 One of the chains was used by workers on the site for haulage, and proved perfectly efficient, before it was realized that it was about 2,000 years old. Some of the remains were of local manufacture, some had come from the Severn area, some from eastern England.

How did this collection—and there is almost certainly a great deal more still unrecovered—come together? There are three possible explanations. One is that this was a sacred site—Posidonius writes of "sacred marshes" in Gaul—and that all the objects found were votive offerings deposited there over a period of 200 years. The second possibility is that they were all pitched there by the Romans after the conquest of Anglesey by Suetonius Paulinus in A.D. 61. A third possibility, and one that is perhaps the most likely, is that some of the objects were votive offerings, and that the remainder were dumped by the Celts themselves before those who could do so escaped to Ireland at the time of the Roman victory.

The druids, one of whose strongholds was Anglesey, date from Celtic times.

On 21st June respectable individuals, wearing what are apparently nightshirts, await the sunrise at Stonehenge. A rival group may be operating on the same day at Tower Hill, while similar if rather more dramatic costumes can be found at the Welsh Eisteddfod. All claim to be druids. Who were the real druids and, more specifically, had they any connection with Stonehenge?

There is a wide gap between the druids-as-known and the druids-as-wished-for. Archaeologists and anthropologists have made a useful distinction between what they term 'hard' and 'soft' primitivists. The hard primitivist examining savage or prehistoric civilization, takes with him as few illusions and preconceived ideas as possible. Not for him the vision of the Golden Age and the Noble Savage. On the contrary, he is inclined to see savage life, in the words of Hobbes, as "solitary, poor, nasty, brutish and short". By contrast, the soft primitivist is a romantic, aware consciously or unconsciously of the imperfection of the society in which he himself lives and eager to recognize the Noble Savage who will provide him with an escape from the intolerable pressure of his own everyday life and with a yardstick by which to measure the inadequacy of that life. Each follows his own line of thought, each gets the Red Indian, the Bedouin, the Druid, that he desires. The more limited the evidence, the greater the room in which to manoeuvre, especially for the soft primitivist. And with the druids the evidence is very sparse: thirty or so fragmentary classical references, a strictly limited quantity of archaeological material, and the survival of analogous types into historical times.

The classical writers often romanticized the Celts, particularly if they had not met them. So Pliny, a scientific observer of the eruption of Vesuvius in A.D. 79, became an unscientific soft primitivist when he described the Celts, who were for him the Hyperboreans (far-northerners). "Their country", he wrote, "is

open to the sun, with a balmy and pleasant climate, without harm-
ful winds or hurtful airs. They live in woods and groves, where
they worship the gods, alone and in groups; and they know no
discord or sickness. . . ." This of life in the damp oakwood forests
of a Sub-Atlantic climate and of men whom those that had met
them regarded as particularly quarrelsome!

The Celtic culture stretched from the Pyrenees to Russia and
northwards to Britain and the North Sea. It was on the whole
coterminous with the temperate deciduous forests—that northern
jungle of monsters and magic which was quite alien to Mediterranean man and which the Celts themselves were busily engaged
in chopping down. The frontiers of this world were being forced
back inexorably as the Roman legions 'pacified' southern France
in 121 B.C., central and northern France by 50 B.C., and southern
Britain by A.D. 47. It was in the course of this advance that the
Romans came in contact with the druids.

Of Celtic temples in Britain there is hardly anything left visible
to the ordinary traveller, though sites have been discovered. They
were small, square enclosures like the one described below at
Maiden Castle. The historical ironist delights to note that, just as
the Romans later planted a Mithraic temple where a twentieth-
century bank would one day stand, so too the best example of a
timber Celtic shrine at present known in England lies hidden
beneath London's Heathrow airport. There post-holes and trenches
marked a rectangular building 18 feet by 15 feet, surrounded by
a colonnade 36 feet by 30.

There are, dotted about the countryside, a number of circular
post-enclosures, which are generally thought to represent the
remains of shrines. At one of these at Frilford, Oxfordshire, there
was found buried within the enclosure a ploughshare together with
a model sword and shields—finds which make a religious purpose
almost a certainty.

At Tara in Ireland the narrow oblong enclosure 750 feet by
90 known as the 'banqueting hall', bears a close resemblance
to two sacred enclosures known to be Celtic which have been
investigated on the Continent, one on the river Marne, the other
in Czechoslovakia.

The origin of the name 'druid' is uncertain. One theory derives
it from the word for an oak together with an element carrying
the meaning 'knowledge'. Certainly knowledge was a key characteristic of the druids. They were the repositories of what was, for
the Celtic world, a corpus of practical information, of essential

Stonehenge, looking south. The entrance to the avenue is in the left foreground. Within the ditch and bank are the white patches marking the Aubrey Holes and two barrows.

Uffington White Horse.

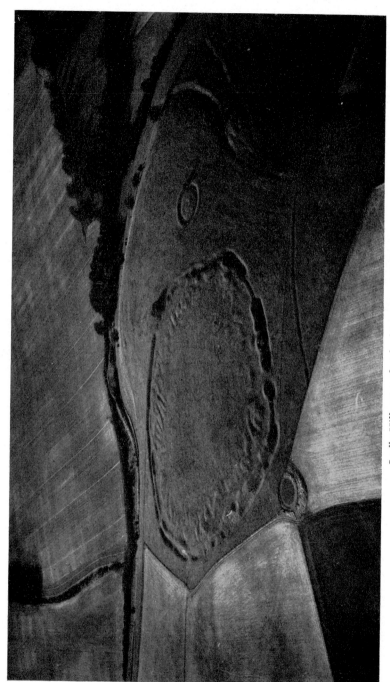

Ladle Hill. an unfinished Iron Age hill-fort.

science; the ways of the gods, the art of poetry, the rhythm of the calendar, the routine of sacrifice and the methods of divination—a group of diverse but closely-linked skills which, as Caesar and other writers agree, took a novitiate of twenty years' duration to acquire.

The Celts believed in a personal immortality—so personal, indeed, that they thought that in the next world they would be able to repay debts contracted in this one. This belief, so different from their own fearful anticipation of an after-life that was flittery and shadowy, was what impressed classical observers. Some confused it with the Pythagorean doctrine of the transmigration of souls, others—nearer the truth—wrote of a Celtic doctrine that the after-life was, as it were, a mirror-image of life on earth.

The druids held the key to this second life; more prosaically, they held the key to this one. Behind the farmer stands the calendar, behind the calendar, the priest. The Celts reckoned by 'a night followed by a day', in contrast with the modern method of reckoning by a day and its following night. A huge bronze calendar, measuring 5 feet by 3 feet 6 inches, found at Coligny in France indicates that they understood the difference between the length of the lunar and solar years and were able to keep the two in step by inserting thirty-day months (instead of their normal twenty-eight-day units) at alternate intervals of two and a half and three years. This method could be run as a nineteen-year cycle. At the end of two such cycles the solar and lunar years would be out of step by only twenty-four hours and could then be brought back into line again by the insertion of a single extra day.

The year was divided into two seasons, warm and cold. It began on 1st November, that turning point in a pastoral-agrarian cycle when those cattle not required for the next year's work are slaughtered. The second festival was on 1st May—the only one which has retained some significance until the present day—when the cattle were turned ont for grazing. Lesser festivals were on the quarter days: 1st February, when the lactation of ewes began; and 1st August, when the crops were ripe for harvesting.

In addition to regulating the calendar, the druids were doctors and soothsayers. Here, too, science shades into magic. Pliny describes their knowledge of curative herbs, which is scientific knowledge, continues with references to the powers of mistletoe, which is magic, but at least definable, and concludes by recounting how he had been shown an anguinam, a magic egg made by the secretions of infuriated snakes—which is not only magic, but also impossible.

Pliny was an accurate observer. Clearly, then, he was shown something natural that he could not identify. What was the anguinam? He describes this magic egg as being round, about the size of an apple, its shell cartilaginous and marked like the arms of an octopus. The marking suggests a sea-urchin. The prime objection to this interpretation is that Pliny would surely have been able to recognize a sea-urchin for what it was. An object is required that was unknown to Mediterranean man. Professor Piggott has suggested that it might have been the empty egg-cases of the whelk *(Buccinum)*, which Pliny might not have known, but which are common in northern Europe. Perhaps, though, they are too common, for the magic apple must surely have been extremely rare, if only because its possession "ensured success' wrote Pliny "in law-courts and before princes"—not a usual experience.

As the transmitters of Celtic knowledge and beliefs the druids symbolized a society at variance in every way with that of the classical world. Moreover, the Romans claimed that human sac-rifice was involved and, cheerfully disregarding their own purpose-less sacrifices of human beings on the altar of pleasure in the amphitheatre, took their stand on their law of 97 B.C. forbidding such sacrifices. The druids were suppressed by Caesar in Gaul, and in Britain their elimination, at least in the lowland zone, followed the Roman conquest. As the embodiment of incomprehensible culture, savage custom and social resistance, there was no place for them in the Roman world. In parts of the highland zone, however, the bards, their successors, survived into comparatively modern times.

There is nothing to connect the druids with Stonehenge. They were rediscovered, so far as England is concerned, and attached to that monument, in the sixteenth and seventeenth centuries. Two developments contributed to this: the Renaissance printing of classical texts revealed their former existence; the discovery of the Red Indian provided a figure which might be equated with an ancient Briton. Thus John Aubrey speculated that the early in-habitants of Britain were "almost as savage as the beasts whose skins were their only raiment. . . . Their priests were Druids. Some of their temples I pretend [claim] to have restored, as Avebury, Stonehenge, &c., as also British sepulchres. . . . They were two

or three degrees, I suppose, less savage than the Americans. . . .
The Romans subdued and civilized them."

It is all there: the juxtaposition of skin-clad Britons and Julius
Caesar, the cross-reference to the Red Indians, and the linking
of the Druids with Stonehenge. Aubrey was not alone in his specu-
lations. The antiquarian eye—and antiquarianism was becoming
fashionable in the seventeenth century—could hardly escape capture by Stonehenge. Inigo Jones was certain that it was all that
remained of a Roman temple, and produced a neat architect's
plan, with three entrances symmetrically placed 120 degrees apart
to show what this temple had been like. Other antiquaries, even
farther off course, believed Stonehenge to be Danish. The layman,
as usual, was confounded by the experts. Walter Pope in "The
Salsbury Ballad" (1676) summed up the situation:

> I will not forget these stones that are set
> In a round on *Salsbury* Plains
> Tho' who brought 'em there, 'tis hard to declare,
> The Romans, or Merlin, or Danes.

Eighteenth-century informed opinion settled firmly for the
druids. In 1740 William Stukeley produced *Stonehenge, a Temple
restor'd to the British Druids*, and followed this three years later
with a similar work on Avebury. Stukeley was, within the limits
of his day, a great archaeologist, but he was not able to stand
outside the preconceptions of that day. He attributed the stones
to the druids who, moreover, he regarded as being of "the patri-
archal religion of Abraham"—by which Stukeley meant, not—as
one might suppose—Jews, but a sort of pre-Christian Christian.

The views of Stukeley and his contemporaries were taken up,
popularized, and in the course of that popularization, debased.
By 1792, Edward Williams, a stone-mason born in 1747 in
Glamorganshire but then working in London, had begun to organize Welsh 'druidic' ceremonies at Primrose Hill. An interesting
sidelight is thrown on his group by the fact that they were ardent
supporters of the French Revolution. One would like to know
more of their social background; it is not the first time that
reforming movements have looked for their pie not in the sky,
not in the future, but in the past. In 1819 Williams was able to
link his movement, which by that time was supported by a large
body of early Welsh texts forged by him personally, to the Welsh
Eisteddfod, which had survived, in an emasculated form, from
earlier days. In 1819 Williams' fictional Gorsedd was united with

the Welsh Eisteddfod at a ceremony held in the grounds of the Ivy Bush Hotel, Carmarthen.

The thing caught on. It was calculated to appeal to the English nineteenth-century view of history as illustrated by such diverse products as the novels of Walter Scott, the paintings of the Pre-Raphaelites, and St. Pancras railway station. Prehistory, too, could be romanticized. Druidic robes and regalia were designed by Sir Hubert Herkomer R.A. and Sir Goscombe John.

Edward Williams had not been alone in his enthusiasm. Everywhere people had been 'discovering' druidic altars. These were often the remains of round barrows, or natural features such as rocking stones. Where nothing suitable existed, something could always be created, as at Ilton in the West Riding. Here William Danby of Swinton Hall had erected in the early nineteenth century a large druidic Folly. Completely spurious, it nevertheless misled some naïve archaeologists and it is well worth seeing. Take road A6108 (Ripon-Richmond) north from Ripon and after about 5 miles turn left through Masham for Ilton, another 3 miles.

From 1781 onwards various groups of 'true' druids have survived in spite of the fissiparous tendency common to this sort of thing. Since 1919 at least five different bodies have laid claim to Stonehenge from which place annually at midsummer dawn English hymn tunes, faintly supported by a harmonium, have faded upon the Wiltshire air. Do not attempt to visit this ceremony. Outsiders became so unpleasant that they are now excluded by the police.

Today the most widespread visible evidence of the Iron Age are the hill-forts, impressive everywhere and common in southern England.

These camps, castles, hill-forts—the names still tend to be used interchangeably, but the last is the most satisfactory—stand out on the Ordnance Survey sheets as irregular enclosures with at least one, and usually two, of their sides following the close-set contour lines of steep slopes. They are the first examples of primarily military architecture in England.

They fall, though this is not always immediately obvious on the map, into three chronological groups, a division reflecting the history of Iron Age Britain. The first invaders constructed enclosures with a single ditch having a counterscarp outside it, a comparatively simple sort of fortification put up between the years 450 and 250 B.C., usually in the earlier part of that period.

In the coastal counties of southern England each block of down-land between one river valley and the next tends to have one of these camps on its heights. There are between thirty and forty examples in Dorset and Hampshire, the most important area.

About 250 B.C. there was an invasion scare as fresh groups, representatives of the La Tène culture that had developed in Europe during the preceding two centuries, reached Britain. The new men were well-equipped with chariots and were intent on conquest. They established their overlordship in Cornwall, in Sussex, and in the east coast lands, especially those of Yorkshire, but, significantly, they by-passed the well-fortified Wessex area. There the old hill-forts were strengthened and new ones were built to repel the invaders. It is to this period that the ditch at Little Woodbury farmstead and the unfinished Ladle Hill fort (see p. 156) belong. In Cornwall the conquerors built their own forts of stone, constructions which today have an uncanny resemblance to the ruins of Norman keeps. In other districts their forts were of a more conventional pattern.

The really dramatic changes in hill-fort construction belong to the late Iron Age, to the forts constructed or re-constructed after 150 B.C. and before the Roman invasion of A.D. 43. During this period there were successive waves of invaders: Belgic refugees from north-east Gaul, following the movement of German tribes into that area, settling in Kent, the coastlands of the Thames estuary and Hertfordshire; the Veneti, refugees from Brittany, following Caesar's campaign there of 56 B.C., landing along the Wessex coast; more Belgic refugees, following the Roman campaigns of 57 to 50 B.C., occupying west Sussex and east Hampshire as far as the river Test.

The new hill-fort pattern was marked by two or three wide rings of banks and ditches, together with maze-like entrances, the fortifications often covering a greater area than the camp which they were designed to defend.

These complexities were a consequence of a change in the method of fighting. The later immigrants, in particular the Veneti from Brittany, were expert with the sling, and they introduced the art of sling-fighting to Wessex. The sling greatly extended the range at which warfare might be carried on. The earlier forts had been intended for defence against the throwing spear, which had a maximum range of about 30 yards. The range of the sling was 100 yards. Hence the multiple ramparts. They held the attacking forces at a distance, while the defenders, firing from above, battered them with stones. Immense quantities of ammunition were stock-piled. At Maiden Castle heaps have been discovered containing between 16,000 and 22,000 slingstones.

The general method of construction of a hill-fort is well understood. First a shallow ditch was dug setting out the shape. The gangs of men started at different points to dig the main ditch, carrying the excavated material inwards to form the main rampart. The outer ditches were cut in the same way. In areas where stone was available, such as Worlebury in Somerset and Chastleton in Oxfordshire, stone walls—or at least walls of stones—were thrown up, and at other sites stones were incorporated in the earth or chalk ramparts. The forts frequently had timber revetments, a timber palisade, and a timber-built gate or gates. The whole structure was a much more business-like affair than the deceptively soft contours surviving today would suggest.

The plan of hill-forts varies somewhat from area to area. The great multivallate hill-forts are, in the south, almost all situated east of the Exe. In Wessex there are about 150 hill-forts, of which a quarter are multivallate. In the south-west peninsula Iron Age forts differ a little from the general pattern. They tend to be of two distinct types. One is the multiple-enclosure fort, in which there is one small inner enclosure and a number of larger outer ones, sometimes arranged concentrically as at Clovelly Dykes. The ramparts are small-scale. These forts are seen as the home of a local chieftain, with enclosures for his stock—and perhaps for the huts of his servants—in the outer precincts. The other type of south-western fort, is a small circular construction with a single rampart. Often known in Cornwall as 'rounds', these forts are probably the defended settlement of a single family group rather than, in the strict sense of the word, a fort.

Iron Age warfare was offensive as well as defensive. Cavalry were not employed, but horses were used for transport and also, more powerfully, harnessed in pairs to fast two-wheeled chariots. The charioteer stood on what was little more than a light wicker platform and was accompanied by his master who was armed with a sword, dagger and two throwing spears—these last rather like a Zulu assegai. There is no evidence for the existence of chariots armed with scythes, as shown in popular pictures and in the Victorian monument commemorating Boadicea at the north end of Westminster Bridge.

Caesar has left the classic description of the tactical use of these chariots. The Britons, he says, would begin by driving their chariots across the battlefield, hurling their throwing spears. Then they would jump down and fight on foot while their chariots, withdrawn a little, provided an easy line of retreat. In this way, he continues with evident admiration, they are able to combine the mobility of cavalry with the fighting power of infantry.

Remains of these chariots have been found, usually in connection with Iron Age burial customs—customs which changed in several ways during the period.

The earlier groups adopted in some areas cremation, in others inhumation, the latter being the more common. The Belgic latecomers practised cremation only. Individual inhumations varied considerably in character. Some were extremely simple, but again there is no general rule.

At Harlyn Bay near Padstow in Cornwall a body was found in a coffin of slate slabs, and there were indications that it had been elaborately adorned with pins, brooches, earrings and a bracelet. These finds are now in the Truro Museum.

At the other end of the kingdom, in Yorkshire, there have been discovered dramatic burials of La Tène aristocrats. The 'Danes'' Graves are in fact an Iron Age cemetery in the East Riding (TA/018633). Turn off road A166 (York-Bridlington) at Driffield, taking B1249 north towards Langtoft. The barrows lies to the east (right-hand) side of this road. There may have been as many as 500 barrows here once, most of them rather poor, but in one of them two men had been buried with the remains of a chariot.

At Arras, just west of Beverley along road A1079 (Beverly-Market Weighton) other chariots have been found. In this cemetery there were about 100 barrows, but three lay apart from the rest. In one of these there had been buried a woman aged about 35. At her head lay her mirror beneath the bones of two pigs. Her body was surrounded by the remains of a chariot, at her back the tyres of the wheels (34 inches in diameter) and before her face the metal pieces of harness from two horses but not the animals themselves. In a second grave there was the skeleton of an old man, parts of a chariot and the remains of the horses. In the third grave there were more pieces from a chariot. The finds are in the British Museum.

There are other chariot burials in Yorkshire, notably one in the North Riding at Cawthorn (SE/784900). Here the woodwork still showed as dust. The wheels were the same diameter as those at Arras and had once had four spokes. The chariot pole between the two horses had extended about 7 feet in front of the chariot itself.

The other source of information about Celtic chariots is the remains found at Llyn Cerrig Bach (see p. 142). Sir Cyril Fox has reconstructed one of these chariots, which can be seen in the National Museum of Wales, Cardiff. In this case the chariot had twelve-spoked wheels, and the yoke poles were of cherrywood or hawthorn.

The Celts went naked into battle, their bodies stained with woad, their main form of protection a large oblong or oval shield. A very fine example was found in the Thames at Battersea, and is now in the British Museum. They used spears and swords, but not the bow and arrow. They shouted battle cries and, at least when fighting among themselves, hurled personal insults and issued individual challenges to their opponents. Frequently they decapitated their opponents, and hung their heads from the bridle of their transport horses. It is probable that these heads also decorated the gates and ramparts of the later forts.

The Iron Age hill-forts and methods of fighting were not proof against the professionalism of the Roman army. During the reconnaissance of 54 B.C. Julius Caesar describes how the soldiers of the Seventh Legion reduced a well-fortified post, the entrances of which had been blocked with felled trees, by locking their shields together over their heads to form a 'tortoise' (testudo) and piling earth against the ramparts. It was only a small fortlet which was overrun on that occasion, but the testudo could just as well provide protection against the slingstones of a giant like Maiden Castle.

Ninety years later, in A.D. 43-4, Vespasian led the Second Augustan Legion in a campaign of conquest across southern England, storming more than twenty hill-forts *en route*. At some of these—for instance Maiden Castle and Spettisbury Rings, both in Dorset—war graves have been discovered where the defeated British had buried their dead. At Spettisbury a skull was recovered with a spearhead still in it, while at Maiden Castle one skeleton had an arrow-head between its ribs and another had been pierced in the head by a square-section bolt from a ballista.

Once taken, the hill-forts lost their original function, but they did not necessarily pass out of use. Some, it is true, were deserted and became farmland, but in others the Romans built their own small, neat, quadrangular forts and signal stations. There is a Roman construction of this type at Hod Hill. In yet others Iron Age civilians squatted throughout the centuries of Roman occupation and on into the post-Roman period.

Of all the hill-forts, Maiden Castle (SY/668885) is the greatest,

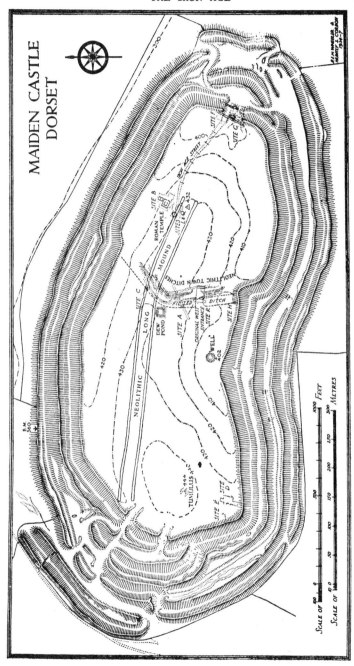

MAIDEN CASTLE
DORSET

though not the grandest, and the most accessible. Moreover, its life spans not just the Iron Age, but a large part of Britain's recent prehistory. Take the Weymouth road out of Dorchester and fork right. A visit to Dorchester Museum is essential. The hill was first settled by Neolithic farmer-pastoralists in the days of the cause-wayed camp. Their enclosure covered about 10 acres and was placed at the east end of the hill, but there is nothing of this to be seen today. A thousand or more years later the immense ridge barrow (see p. 60) was constructed. After a few more centuries a Bronze Age round barrow was raised to the south of it and this is still conspicuous.

Another 1,000 years passed and an Iron Age hill-fort was built, which overlay the Neolithic causewayed camp. It had entrances at the east and west end, a rampart 10 feet high and 12 feet wide revetted with timber, and a ditch 50 feet wide and 20 feet deep. An interesting feature was a cobbled area outside the eastern entrance, its purpose unknown, but conceivably the site of a cattle market.

Early in the second century B.C. the whole of the hill was enclosed with a bank and ditch, making a 'town' of about 45 acres, where a comparatively large number of people lived in huts of wood and stone linked by stone tracks and surrounded by a jumble of pits for food storage and rubbish disposal.

In the first century B.C. the final reconstruction took place. Defence in depth was now the necessity. Another ditch and bank were added to the entire camp, the entrances were turned into complex mazes, the east gateway was furnished with piles of slingstones and platforms were put up for the slingers, the gateway itself was revetted with stone brought from Upwey 2 miles to the south, and sentry boxes were built.

There are signs that about A.D. 25 these defences were repaired. The interior of the town was tidied up and the tracks were resurfaced. But within twenty years Maiden Castle had fallen to the Romans. Vespasian stormed it during his march westwards across southern England. The fiercest fighting seems to have taken place around the great east gate, and it was just outside this gate that the British war graves were dug.

After the conquest the Romans created a new local centre down in the valley at Dorchester (Durnovaria) and, for perhaps the first time in 3,000 years, Maiden Castle was unoccupied. The interior was ploughed up—it was at this time that the ridge barrow virtually disappeared.

However, that was not quite the end of the story. About the years 350 to 370 an oval hut, a two-roomed house and a small Romano-British temple were put up at the eastern end of the hill. The ruined eastern gate was provided with mortared stone-work and a stone track led up to the temple, which was itself surrounded by a wooden fence. It was a simple room, only 16 feet square, with a floor of brick mosaic squares (tesserae) and plastered walls. There was a veranda. To this sanctuary the peasants of Dorchester came and paid their civilized respects to the figures of a three-horned bull, of Diana and of Minerva, which are now in the museum at Dorchester. The oval hut may have preserved the site of an earlier, Iron Age shrine. The priest lived in the little house behind the temple. There was, for a time, peace.

Maiden Castle is the Stonehenge or the New Grange of hill-forts, but there are many other sites which are, for one reason or another, worth visiting.

On the Cotswolds there is Old Sodbury (ST/761826), a quarter of a mile to the west of road A46 (Bath-Stroud), a good, clear, accessible example, 24 acres in area, with walls that were partly rebuilt by the Romans. At Bristol, in Leigh Woods just to the west of the Suspension Bridge, there is Stokeleigh (ST/559733), picturesque, and interesting because part of the stone-facing of its walls has been cleared. Walls of tumbled stone can be seen at Worlebury (ST/314625), covering 10½ acres on the north side of Weston-super-Mare; and at Dolebury (ST/450589), just east of road A38 (Bridgwater-Bristol) and 14 miles south of Bristol, a nice fort covering 22½ acres. The cuttings inside are much later in date, the result of lead-mining—and perhaps of treasure-seeking, for

> If Dolebury digged were
> Of gold should be the share

they say. But if Dolebury has any gold, it is still there.

Ham Hill (ST/485165), 5 miles west of Yeovil and to the south of road A3088 (Yeovil-Ilminster) where it passes through Stoke sub Hamdon, is probably the largest hill-fort in Britain, covering about 200 acres. The ditches are double—triple to the south west and north east—and were cut into the living rock. The fort was probably occupied throughout the Iron Age and on into Roman times, when Ham stone, famous as a building material, was quarried there.

Badbury Rings (ST/964030), 3½ miles north-west of Wimborne Minster on the north side of B3082 (Blandford-Forum-Wimborne

Minister), has three circular banks and ditches, an elaborate western entrance and a staggered eastern one, and encloses about 20 acres. It is rather heavily-wooded, but is worth the struggle. At the north-west edge of the outermost bank there can be seen a clear stretch of Ackling Dyke. This is a part of the Roman road that ran from Salisbury to Vinocladia close by, about 40 feet wide and 6 feet high, with its banks and ditches set back on either side.

Ladle Hill (SU/478568), 2 miles north-east of Litchfield in Hampshire, is the classic example of an unfinished fort, a site that enables the method of construction to be clearly seen. Litchfield is on road A34 (Winchester-Newbury). Sections of half-dug ditch can still be seen, each worked on by different gangs of men and not yet joined up. Further in towards the centre the piles of turf and topsoil removed from the ditch were dumped, being left there to face the rampart of chalk rubble that was never constructed. The war-scare passed, and perhaps it was felt that the labour involved in constructing these small forts—Ladle Hill is only about 7 acres in extent—was not worthwhile.

Uffington Castle (SU/299864) in Berkshire can be conveniently combined with the White Horse and the earlier Wayland's Smithy. It should be avoided, though, at weekends. The fort covers about 8 acres—something of about this area seems to have been a standard size for the smaller forts—and has a bank, ditch and counterscarp. The bank was strengthened by having sarsens built into it and timber posts. Uffington can be reached by taking B3507 (Swindon-Wantage) and turning south at the signpost 6 miles from Wantage.

Tournerbury (SZ/73 99) is one for the collectors only. There is not much to see, but it is one of the very few 'hill' forts that is not on a hill, being on the contrary at sea-level on Hayling Island, Hampshire. Again the area is about 8 acres.

Three of the most rewarding forts are in Dorset at Abbotsbury, Hambledon Hill and Hod Hill. Abbotsbury Castle (SY/556865) lies to the north side of B3157 (Bridport-Abbotsbury) about 2 miles from Abbotsbury itself. It is a triangular fort of about 5 acres, with triple ramparts on the accessible south-east side. Within the fort there are three features of interest: a Bronze Age round barrow at the highest point; the remains of ten hut platforms on the north-east slope; and a small rectangular enclosure in the south-west corner. This is probably a Roman signal station, built after the conquest. A bonus is the superb view on a clear day over the west end of Chesil Bank and out across the Channel.

Hambledon Hill (ST/845126) and Hod Hill (ST/857106) lie to the west of road A350 (Blandford Forum-Shaftesbury). Take the secondary road to the west 4 miles out of Blandford towards the delightfully-named Child Okeford. This passes between the two camps, Hod Hill to the south, Hambledon to the north.

Hod Hill covers about 50 acres and has several special features. The south-east corner (the site is rectangular) has not been cultivated, and there are the remains of about fifty hut circles and 100 pits. Probably the rest of the site was also occupied. The Romans attacked the settlement with ballista bolts. After the capture and slaughter of the inhabitants, the victors built a square fort in the north-west corner. This was a large affair, providing accommodation for 600 legionaries and 250 cavalry. At the centre were the headquarters (principia) and commandant's quarters. There were stables at the north-west gate and a cistern cut out of the chalk, capable of holding nearly 2,000 gallons. Just outside the north-west gate there is an enclosure which may have been the commandant's garden. The fort itself was built at the time of the conquest, and was originally constructed of timber, wattle and daub. It was probably employed as a base from which to supervise the natives when nearby areas were being developed as grain-producing estates worked by British slave labour.

On the other side of the valley Hambledon Hill fort has triple ramparts, except on its south side, which enclose 25 acres. Within there are about 200 hut platforms and several sunken tracks. Signs of some of these remains can be seen when the sun is low. Hambledon is less interesting than Hod Hill, but it seems a pity to miss it, when it lies only a mile or so away across the road.

South Cadbury (ST/628251) in Somerset lies half a mile south of road A303 (Sparkford-Wincanton) about 2 miles east of Sparkford. The camp, Cadbury Castle, is just beyond the church. Here recent excavations have demonstrated an almost continuous use of the site from Neolithic times down to the close of the Saxon period, a length of time measuring 4,000 years. In the sixteenth century Leland recorded that "gold, sylver and coper of the Romayne coynes and Many Antique Thinges" had been found there, and legend has persistently identified the fort with Arthur's Camelot. The king and his knights can still be seen when the moon is full, it is said, riding on silver-shod horses along the line to the north-west of the camp marked on the Ordnance map as King Arthur's Causeway. Excavations recently completed—the site can be visited—indicate that it was at least a Dark Age stronghold of considerable importance. The camp has quadruple banks and ditches enclosing an area of 18 acres.

Apart from the Midland area—always a blank—there are few counties without an Iron Age hill-fort worth a visit. This being so, any short list will seem partial, nevertheless a personal selection of twenty Iron Age hill-camps not mentioned in the text is:

Cambridgeshire: Wandlebury (TL/494534), north side of A604 Cambridge-Linton).

Cheshire: Castle Ditch (SJ/553695), 2 miles north-east of Kelsall, A54 (Chester-Winsford).

Cornwall: Carn Brae (SW/686407), south of A30 (Camborne-Redruth).

Derbyshire: Mam Tor (SK/128837), 1½ miles west of Castleton A625 (Chapel en le Frith-Sheffield).

Herefordshire: Croft Ambry (SO/444668), Yatton, east of A4110 (Knighton-Mortimer's Cross).

Kent: Oldbury (TQ/582562), on north side of A25 (Sevenoaks-Ightham).

Leicestershire: Burrough Hill (SK/761119), west of A606 (Melton Mowbray-Oakham).

Northumberland: Yeavering Bell (NT/928294), west of A697 (Wooler-Coldstream).

Shropshire: Old Oswestry (SJ/296310), one mile north of Oswestry (A483).

Surrey: Anstiebury (TQ/153441), 3 miles south of Dorking (A24).

Sussex: Cissbury (TQ/139081), east of A24 (Worthing-Horsham), finds in museums at Worthing and Brighton.

Wiltshire: Yarnbury (SU/035404), north side of A303 (Wincanton-Amesbury), finds in museum at Devizes.

Worcestershire: Bredon Hill (SO/958402), east of A38 (Tewkesbury-Worcester).

In Wales hill-forts abound. Among the best are:

NORTH WALES

Caernarvonshire: Tr'er Ceiri (SH/373446), on the summit of Yr Eifl, west of A499 (Caernarvon-Pwllheli).

Denbighshire: Parc y Meirch (SH/968756), Dinorben (A548).

Flintshire: Pen y Cloddiau (SJ/130675), west of A341 (Mold-Denbigh).

Merionethshire: Pen y Dinas (SH/606208), east of A496 (Barmouth-Llanbedr).

SOUTH WALES

Brecknockshire: Castell Dinas (SO/178302), east of A479 (Talgarth-Crickhowell).

Carmarthenshire: Carn Goch (SN/691243), west of A4069 (Llan-dovery-Brynamman).
Pembrokeshire: Moel Trigarn (SN/158336), west of A478 (Cardigan-Narberth).

With the Roman storming of Maiden Castle and the Saxon occupation of Cadbury one has clearly crossed the frontier that separates history from prehistory. Iron Age independence and, in a formal sense, British prehistory, were together brought to an end, at least in lowland Britain, by the Roman Conquest.

The final phase of the Iron Age lasted for about 100 years. In 55 and 54 B.C. Julius Caesar mounted two reconnaissance expeditions in the course of which he encountered unexpected difficulties at sea from the tides and currents of the Channel and on land from the British chariots. The expeditions were, however, in his eyes no more than isolated incidents in his successful conquest of Gaul.

The Belgic invasions of about 75 B.C. had led to the establishment of an aggressive statelet in Kent and, later, Hertfordshire and Essex, that of the Catuvellauni, 'the Mighty Warriors'. It was this state with which Caesar came in contact, ruled at the time by Cassivellaunus—the first person in Britain whose name we know. In the course of Caesar's second expedition the Catuvellaunnian capital at Wheathampstead, "a place of great natural strength and well-fortified" was taken and sacked.

To the east of Wheathampstead (TL/184135) there are sections of a bank and ditch which probably represent the defences of the capital. Wheathampstead lies east of road A6 between Luton and St. Albans.

It was as a consequence of Caesar's Gallic wars that another Belgic leader, Commius, ruler of the Atrebates, fled to Britain (*c.* 52 to 50 B.C.) and set up a powerful state in Hampshire, with its capital at Silchester. Silchester is today the site of the fascinating remains of a Roman town, but the earlier Belgic fortifications are not noticeable at ground level.

Between the Roman reconnaissance under Caesar and the conquest 100 years later there was a great deal of friction between the Belgic state based on Silchester and that of the Catuvellauni with the latter apparently the more aggressive and the more powerful. Their great ruler was Cunobelin, Shakespeare's Cymbeline, who ruled from about A.D. 10 to 41. The tribal capital was now at Colchester (TL/997253) in Essex, which became, after its conquest, the first Roman capital (Camulodunum) of their new province. Finds from both periods are in the Colchester Museum.

Colchester had been set up originally by the Trinovantes, whose appeal to Caesar for protection from the onslaughts of the Mighty Warriors, their western neighbours, had been one of the reasons for his two reconnaissance expeditions, but by A.D. 24 Cunobelin had conquered the Trinovantes and had also overrun Kent.

In consequence Cunobelin felt himself justified in taking the proud title Rex Britannorum, King of the Britons. The transference of his capital to Colchester was not only a symbol of his conquest of the Trinovantes, it was also a move to a fine defensive site. Modern developments have not entirely concealed the fact that Colchester is defended by water on three sides. At Wivenhoe about 4 miles to the south-east, the river Colne divides. The Colne itself flows round the north side of the town, while the significantly named Roman River covers the southern approaches. There are a series of ditches and banks in the area to the west and south of the modern town which protect this easily defensible area: Gryme's Dyke (TL/956267), Tripple Dyke (TL/963260), Lexden Dyke (TL/978270), Berechurch Dyke (TL/997203), and Sheepen Dyke (TL/985257).

This last can not be seen at ground level, but it was in this area that Cunobelin had his capital, now farm-land. After the Roman Conquest the capital was destroyed and the Roman town built just to the east, where modern Colchester stands. The builders of the new town used the site of the old one for kilns and workshops.

Cunobelin had died a few years before the conquest, in A.D. 41. There is in Lexden Park a barrow known as Lexden Tumulus (TL/975247) which is almost certainly the grave of Cunobelin himself. The rich remains—most of them deliberately damaged as part of the burial ceremony—are now in the town museum.

During 100 years between the expeditions of Caesar and the Roman Conquest there had been increasing trade and contact between Britain and the Roman Empire, which now suddenly faced it across a narrow stretch of water. In Roman eyes Britain was a source of actual unrest and of potential wealth; the first assumption was true, the second largely false.

In the reign of the emperor Claudius (A.D. 41 to 54) it was decided to conquer the island. Forty-one years later the Romans had pacified the lowlands and had penetrated into the highlands of Scotland.

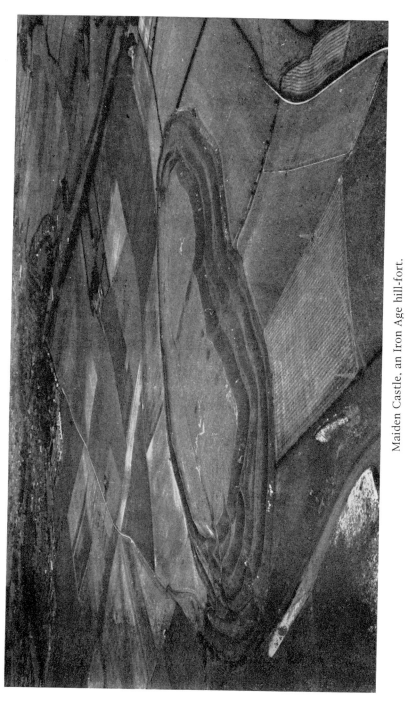

Maiden Castle, an Iron Age hill-fort.

Chysauster, Romano-British courtyard houses. *(above)* An aerial view. *(below)* The courtyard of one house, with rooms and outbuildings in the surrounding wall.

It was in A.D. 43 that Claudius despatched an army of 40,000 men under the command of Aulus Plautius. Sailing from Boulogne they landed at Richborough in Kent. The chief of West Sussex became a client king, and the Catuvellauni, led by Cunobelin's sons, Togodumnus and the more able Caratacus, were defeated, the latter only after a two-day battle—an event almost unique in those days—at the Medway in the neighbourhood of Rochester. West Sussex, Kent and Essex provided a 'beachhead'. Phase one of the conquest was over.

Phase two followed at once. From the base which they had secured in the south-east, the Romans launched a three-pronged advance across the lowland zone.

The Ninth Legion moved north to what is now Lincoln. Their route is marked by the supply road which is today known as Ermine Street, approximately followed from London by, successively, roads A10, A14, A1, as far as Water Newton. Beyond that village the road ran across country through Bourne and Ancaster to Lincoln itself.

In the centre the Fourteenth Legion, and perhaps also the Twentieth, followed the Midland way later called Watling Street— the modern A5—as far as High Cross, south-west of Leicester.

The Second Legion had the hardest task, fighting its way south-west, capturing the Isle of Wight, and storming twenty hill-camps *en route* to some point beyond Maiden Castle. Their supply route eventually ran through Silchester and Old Sarum (Salisbury) to Dorchester—approximately A30 and A354.

By A.D. 47 the lowland zone south of the Trent and east of the Severn was securely held. The lead mines of Mendip were already operating under Roman control, while the cornlands of Salisbury Plain and Cranborne Chase, the granary of Iron Age Britain, were in the process of being turned into imperial estates to feed the Roman army of occupation. Phase two had been completed.

The limit of the conquered zone was marked by another road, part frontier-line, part supply-route for the troops, the Fosse Way. This road ran from Seaton on the south Devon coast, the first base of the Second Legion, through High Cross, to Lincoln, the base of the Ninth. In due course it was extended to Exeter, while the Twentieth and Fourteenth Legions were stationed in forward positions at Gloucester and Wroxeter respectively.

All was not secure, however. After the battle of the Medway Caratacus had escaped to Wales, where he organized the resistance of the southern people, the Silures. In A.D. 50 troops from

Gloucester drove him north. In North Wales he again led the resistance, this time of the Ordovices, from whose area he was driven out by the Romans in the following year.

Caratacus now moved to the territory of the unconquered Brigantes of north-east England—and their queen, Cartimandua, to her eternal shame, handed him over to the Romans, who marched him in chains with his wife and children through the streets of Rome. There Tacitus records that he refused to beg for mercy. He asked instead "Because you want to rule the world, does it follow that the world wants to be enslaved by you?" He was a great resistance leader, insufficiently honoured today in his own country.

Caratacus had shown the Romans that new campaigns were called for. To the west, Wales threatened the security of the conquered lowlands, while in the north Cartimandua, that friendly ruler, was overthrown and forced to seek the protection of the Romans.

In A.D. 71 the Brigantes were defeated, and their huge camp at Stanwick was taken by forces operating from the new Roman base at York. Wales was conquered between A.D. 74 and 78, new legionary bases being established at Caerleon in the south and Chester in the north. Then, between 79 and 83 Agricola secured southern Scotland and advanced up the east coast almost as far as Inverness. An advance base was built at Inchtuthil (NO/125397), to reach which turn south from road A984 about half way between Dunkeld and Coupar Angus. This fort covered 50 acres and was large enough to house a legion, but by the close of the century the Romans had withdrawn, temporarily, to the Tyne-Solway line marked by Hadrian's Wall, itself constructed during the years A.D. 122 to 136.

Celtic civilization did not come to an end with the Roman Occupation. In Wales it survived until the Norman Conquest of 1066–1100. In Scotland Alexander III was the last king to be inaugurated in the traditional manner. That was in 1249. In Ireland the Elizabethans encountered, and cruelly destroyed, a Celtic way of life. The last Gaelic lordship there was that of Domhnaill in 1592. In the islands off Ireland and Scotland, Celtic society lasted much longer.

Two Iron Age features of the early Roman period are well worth a visit, one in the north and one in the south of England.

In Yorkshire there is the Brigantian fort at Stanwick (NZ/

180115). From Richmond in the North Riding follow B6274 for about 5 miles. At Forcett, take the minor road east towards Aldborough St. John. The site lies between this village and Forcett. It can be approached equally well by turning west off B6275 to Aldborough and going on from there towards Caldwell and Forcett. Most of the finds are in the British Museum, but some are in the museum at York.

The kingdom of the Brigantes stretched from the Humber in the south to Durham in the north, while loosely-attached allies extended the Brigantian sphere of influence to Dumfries and to parts of Lancashire.

The queen of this apparently powerful state, Cartimandua, had, as has been already noticed, collaborated with the Romans. Her husband, Venutius, supported the resistance movement. He seized power and began to develop the defences at Stanwick. A period of civil war was followed by a brief peace, broken when Cartimandua took her husband's armour-bearer to her bed. She fled south and Venutius resumed his preparations to meet the Romans.

The original fort at Stanwick had covered 17 acres. It lies to the south-west of Stanwick Church and is surrounded by ramparts 24 feet from ditch to crest. This first enclosure had been built before the events just described, perhaps soon after the original Roman invasion of A.D. 43.

About A.D. 50 to 60 Stanwick was extended to the north to take in a water supply—part of the Mary Wild Beck—and a further 130 acres of land. The new walls were revetted with drystone work to a height of 15 feet and achieved a total height of 28 feet from ditch to crest.

Finally, about A.D. 70, another 600 acres was added, mainly to the south of the existing stronghold. This huge construction— the total area enclosed was about one square mile—was never completed. Around the southern gate (in the middle of the south bank) chunks of stone still lay in 1950 where they had been hastily left almost 1,900 years earlier when the camp was stormed by the Romans. The legions then involved were the Twentieth, under the great Agricola, and the Ninth.

Excavation has revealed a high proportion of pottery from south-east England and of red Samian ware from Gaul, indicating large-scale trade with these areas. A pool of brackish water near the western entrance preserved a wooden bowl of oak, some basket-work, and a sword still in its scabbard of ash. Close by lay a skull with sword cuts across the eye socket and forehead and with

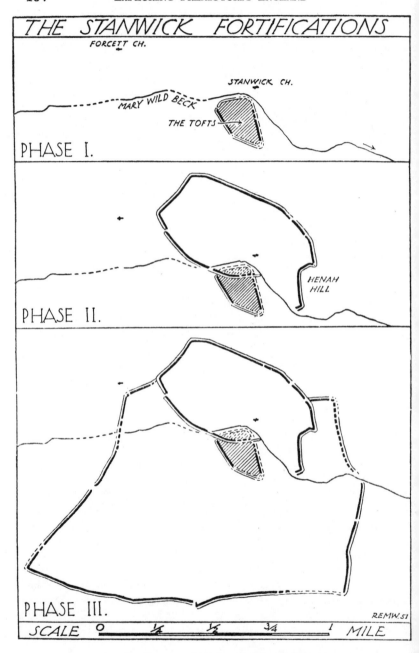

THE STANWICK FORTIFICATIONS

FORCETT CH.

STANWICK CH.

MARY WILD BECK

THE TOFTS

PHASE I.

HENAH HILL

PHASE II.

PHASE III.

REMW.51

SCALE   0   ¼   ½   ¾   1   MILE

(Reproduced by permission of the Society of Antiquaries of London)

clear indications that it had been cut off below the fourth vertebra.

If Stanwick in the north provides evidence of the military conquest of Celts by Romans, Chysauster in the extreme south-west shows evidence of a different sort of conquest, being an example of cultural imitation.

Chysauster (SW/473350) lies north of Trevarrack off B3311 (Penzance-St. Ives). Here there is a Romano-British settlement of about the first century A.D. Some of the finds are in the museums at Penzance and Truro. Four pairs of houses stand on either side of a paved street. Behind the houses were vegetable gardens and from the village a road led down to the stream below. The houses were so arranged that they faced away from the driving south-west Atlantic gales.

The buildings at Chysauster are courtyard-houses, that is to say the dwelling place and the outbuildings are constructed as an organic unit, built out of a single surrounding wall and giving onto a central courtyard. The design is apparently confined to the Land's End peninsula. It looks as though its origins may have been two-fold. On the one hand, some of the much earlier Dartmoor dwellings, such as those of Dean Moor (see p. 117), had been constructed out of a retaining wall, while on the other hand the arrangement around the central courtyard suggests a crude imitation of the disposition of rooms in a typical Roman house.

The houses are roughly circular, about 80 feet in diameter, with the living quarters opposite the entrance. On either side of these are enclosures used as workrooms or as shelters for stock. One of the houses (number three) seems to have been double and was probably the home of the head-man.

A number of these little settlements have been discovered in the Land's End area, for instance at Sancreed (SW/402289), north of road A30 (Penzance-Land's End), and at Porthmeor (SW/428370), south of B3306 (St. Ives-St. Just).

At Chysauster there are two or three huts lying outside the village and sharing a fogou. The fogou is peculiar to the Land's End sites. It consists essentially of a stone-lined underground tunnel, with variations in detail. Sometimes the tunnel is open at both ends, sometimes only at one; sometimes it begins in the courtyard of a house, as at Sancreed, sometimes in a fort, as at St. Hiliary. A large fogou may be 20 or 30 feet long and 5 or 6 feet wide. The fogou at Carn Euny, Sancreed, is a particularly nice one.

Originally it was believed that the fogous were hiding-places in times of danger, but they are not concealed and to take refuge in one would be to enter a trap. Today it is thought that they served the much less romantic function of a larder. These primitive refrigerators are normally orientated north-east and south-west. The prevailing wind would have blown through them, while the rain could have been kept out. In some places their floor has been found to be covered with a layer of charcoal and bones.

In the magnitude of its effect on the culture of the lowland zone the Roman Occupation, though it only endured for three centuries, is comparable with those much earlier critical shifts, the retreat of the Ice Sheet, the opening of the English Channel, and the Neolithic agricultural revolution.

There is growing evidence that the pattern imposed by that occupation left behind it a lasting impression not only by the creation of towns and the construction of roads which have survived to the present day, but also in patterns of rural agriculture. Most important of all, the last of the prehistoric societies, that of the Iron Age, was overlaid with a lasting tincture of something new, the way of life of the urban, slave-owning, legalistic Roman Empire.

THE TREASURES OF TIME

The piecing together of the story behind the visible fragments of prehistory—"fragments corroded" as William Stukeley wrote, "like wormeaten wood by the harsh jaws of time"—is itself a lengthy process which has already occupied 400 years.

Before the sixteenth century the more dramatic remains were naturally the objects of wonder, superstition or fear. Sometimes these were recorded, as in the comments on Stonehenge (see Chapter VI), or survived in folk memory, as in the legends attached to Wayland's Smithy (see Chapter III).

Often dread or admiration is enshrined in the mere names themselves by which the remains are still known today. Heroes and villains are credited with constructions from end to end of England: Arthur's Stone; Robin Hood's Butts; Danes' Graves, Caesar's Camp—behind these names are concealed a chambered long barrow, Bronze Age round barrows, an Iron Age cemetery and an Iron Age hill-camp.

Less obvious is the fear behind the cluster of names such as Grime's Graves, Grim's Ditch, Grim's Dyke, Grimspound. Grim, a name for the Norse god Woden, meant in its general sense "the person who conceals his name" and became a periphrasis for the Devil—who also appears without an alias in names like the Devil's Arrows, the Devil's Bed and Bolster, the Devil's Dyke, the Devil's Humps, the Devil's Jumps, the Devil's Ring and the Devil's Quoits. Hidden behind this common attribution are, respectively, standing stones in Yorkshire, a long barrow in Somerset, an Iron Age hill-camp, two sets of Bronze Age round barrows, a Bronze Age saucer-barrow and a Bronze Age sanctuary.

More prosaically, to the Saxons many remains were either shelters (Coldharbour) or fortified places (burhs) as indicated by the large number of prehistoric sites ending in -borough, -burrow, or -bury, such as Lamborough Banks, Burrow Camp and Gorsey Bigbury, which name a long barrow, a henge monument and an Iron Age hill-camp.

Mention of the most outstanding places such as Stonehenge occurs in medieval chronicles, but it was in the sixteenth and early seventeenth centuries that there appeared a more considered interest and a more accurate description of 'ancient remains'. This sprang partly from the intellectual climate, which might be described as watered-down Renaissance, and partly from more mundane, though related, factors such as the dissolution of the monasteries, which provided the original impetus for John Leland's *Description of the Realm of England, c.* 1540. Leland told Henry VIII how he became "totally inflamed with a love to see thoroughly all those parts of this your opulent and ample realm that I had read of" and how he "noted in so doing a whole world of things very memorable". The development of land-surveying and the construction of accurate maps led inevitably to a consideration of prehistoric features, and the more striking of these found their way into the text of Speed's great *Theatre of the Empire of Great Britain* (1611). On the back of the Cornish plate for instance, there is, under the heading *Memorable Things*: "At *Boskenna* upon the South-west of her *Promontorie*, is a *Trophy* erected, which are eighteene Stones placed round in compasse, and pitched twelve foot each from others, with another farre bigger in the very center. These doe shewe some Victorie there attained either by the *Romans*, or else King *Athelstane*."

During the seventeenth century the approach became increasingly one of unprejudiced examination. Inigo Jones might be so sure that Stonehenge was a Roman temple that even he, an architect, was blinded to the actual details of its construction (1620), but Sir Thomas Browne (1605–82) and John Aubrey (1626–97) were more detached. Aubrey has already been quoted. Sir Thomas Browne wrote two papers on 'Urns' found in Norfolk and managed to combine superb prose rhythms with accurate observation. He was able to write: "The treasures of time lie high, in Urnes, Coynes, and Monuments, scarce below the roots of some vegetables. Time hath endlesse rarities, and shows of all varieties; which reveals old things in heaven, makes new discoveries in earth, and even earth itself a discovery. That great Antiquity *America* lay buried for a thousand years; and a large part of the earth is still in the Urne unto us."

But also:

> Of these Pots none were found above Three Quarters of a Yard
> in the Ground, whereby it appeareth, that in all this Time the
> Earth hath little varied its Surface, though this Ground hath been
> plowed to the utmost Memory of Man. Whereby it may also be
> conjectured, that this hath not been a Wood-Land, as some con-
> ceive all this Part to have been; for in such Lands they usually
> made no common Burying-places, except for some special Persons
> in graves, and likewise that there hath been an Ancient Habitation
> about these Parts; for at Buxton also, not a Mile off, urnes have
> been found in my Memory, but in their Magnitude, Figure, Colour,
> Posture, &c., there was no small Variety, some were large and
> capacious, able to contain abot Two Gallons, some of a middle,
> others of a smaller Size; the great ones probably belonging to
> greater Persons, or might be Family Urnes, fit to receive the Ashes
> successively of their Kindred and Relations, and therefore of these,
> some had Coverings of the same Matter, either fitted to them, or a
> thin flat stone, like a Grave Slate, laid over them. . . .

In the eighteenth century two lines of approach are discernible.
On the one hand, there was the increasingly rational, scientific
attitude of men like William Stukeley (1687–1765). He has already
been referred to in earlier chapters, but one must quote his
reference to crop markings, one of the bases of twentieth-century
aerial archaeology. In Essex Stukeley observed "the perfect vestigia
of a temple, as easily discernible in the corn as upon paper",
adding that the locals told him that "let the year come as it will,
this place is ever visible, and that it has been so ever since the
memory of man", and that they believed it to be produced by the
fairies dancing.

The other line of eighteenth-century archaeological activity
was less desirable. In the later years and on into the nineteenth
century, to excavate became an entertainment to occupy a summer
afternoon or two. The leisured sat and enjoyed their cold chicken
and claret, while the servants opened some 'tumulus' or other. If
anything were found, it graced the country gentleman's showcase
of curiosities.

Meanwhile the rough outline of a scientific framework was being
drawn. The word 'prehistory' appears to have been first used by
a Frenchman in 1833. In Denmark the three age system of Stone,
Bronze and Iron which still provides a rough—though increasingly
unsatisfactory—scheme of reference today, was outlined by a
writer in 1813. Speaking of the inhabitants of Scandinavia, Vedel-

Simonsen observed: " . . . the development of their culture can be divided into a Stone Age, a Copper Age and an Iron Age. These three ages cannot be separated from each other by exact limits, for they encroach on each other. Without any doubt the use of stone implements continued among the more impoverished groups after the introduction of copper, and similarly objects of copper were used after the introduction of iron. . . ." Three years later show-cases in the Danish National Museum were arranged on these lines.

The literal interpretation of the Bible, which placed the origin of the universe less than 6,000 years earlier, checked the development of any scheme of extended chronology, but this interpretation was weakened about the middle of the nineteenth century. In so far as England was concerned, this was achieved by geological arguments outlined by Sir Charles Lyell (1797–1875) as early as 1830–33, and by Charles Darwin 1809–92) in his *The Origin of Species by Natural Selection* (1859) and *The Descent of Man* (1871).

Practical archaeology advanced as fast as, or faster than, theoretical work. The great name here, at least as far as north-western European excavations are concerned, is that of General Pitt-Rivers (1827–1900). He had all the qualifications: a considerable private income, the absolute ownership of large areas of Cranborne Chase rich in remains, and a methodical no-nonsense approach to problems which was partly temperamental and partly acquired during his service in the army.

Pitt-Rivers described his principles in a series of books *Excavations in Cranborne Chase*, published during the period 1887–1898:

> Excavators, as a rule, record only those things which appear to them important at the time, but fresh problems in Archaeology and Anthropology are constantly arising, and it can hardly fail to have escaped the notice of anthropologists, especially those who, like myself, have been concerned with the morphology of art, that, on turning back to old accounts in search of evidence, the points which would have been most valuable have been passed over from being thought uninteresting at the time. Every detail should, therefore, be recorded in the manner most conducive to facility of reference, and it ought at all times to be the chief object of an excavator to reduce his own personal equation to a minimum.

> I have endeavoured to record the results of these excavations in such a way that the whole of the evidence may be available for those who are concerned to go into it. . . . Much of what is recorded may never prove of further use, but even in the case of

such matter, superfluous precision may be regarded as a fault on the right side where the arrangement is such as to facilitate reference and enable a selection to be made. A good deal of rash and hasty generalization of our time arises from the unreliability of the evidence upon which it is based. It is next to impossible to give a continuous narrative of any archaeological investigation that is entirely free from bias; undue stress will be laid upon facts that seem to have an important bearing upon theories that are current at the time, whilst others that might come to be considered of greater value afterwards are put in the background or not recorded, and posterity is endowed with a legacy of error that can never be rectified. . . .

A tumulus is easily dug into, and the relics obtained from it are of value, whereas the examination of a town or encampment is a costly undertaking, and the relics have seldom any intrinsic value, consisting mostly of common objects that have been thrown away by the inhabitants. It is for this reason that our knowledge of pre-historic and early people is derived chiefly from their funeral deposits, and for all we know of their mode of life, excepting such information as has been obtained from lake dwellings, and cran-nogs, they might as well have been born dead.

Written eighty and more years ago, these extracts from General Pitt-Rivers' volumes would still obtain general acceptance from professional archaeologists (a notoriously contumacious group) to-day. Archaeology had come of age.

Yet there was, naturally, a chronological overlap with the earlier centuries of fancy, gullibility and deception. In this connec-tion the story of Piltdown man (1912–1953) is interesting, comic, mysterious.

Piltdown (TQ/439217) is in Sussex on road A272 east of Hay-wards Heath. There is an inn, "The Piltdown Man". Beside a gravel pit about a mile away there still is recorded: "Here in the old river gravel Mr. Charles Dawson FSA found the fossil skull of Piltdown man 1912–13. The discovery was described by Mr. Charles Dawson and Sir Arthur Smith Woodward in the Quarterly Journal of the Geological Society 1913–15."

Charles Dawson was a solicitor in Uckfield and an expert amateur geologist and archaeologist. He had made a number of small but valuable discoveries. Smith Woodward was a professional geologist employed by the British Museum and a personal friend of Dawson's.

On 18th December 1912, Dawson and Woodward told the Geological Society about Dawson's latest and greatest discovery.

A few years earlier, Dawson said, he had been given by labourers digging in the gravel pit "an unusually thick" piece of skull, and "some years later, in the Autumn of 1911" he had himself picked up another piece. By the time of the meeting Dawson had collected several pieces of skull and part of a jaw-bone with two molars in it. The skull appeared rather human, the jaw appeared ape-like, the two molars were more human than ape-like.

At this time theories concerning man's possible ancestors were dominated by the idea of what was vulgarly called 'the missing link', a hypothetical common ancestor of apes and men. It was assumed that he would have a skull-case that inclined towards the human and a jaw that was more ape-like. Dawson's discoveries were exactly what professionals were expecting to find. A link had been recovered, *Eoanthropus dawsoni*, the dawn man of Dawson, the Piltdown Man.

Other discoveries followed—teeth, bones, an elephant bone shaped into a tool, part of another skull from a site *2 miles away* from the first. In 1909 Dawson had written to Woodward that he was "waiting for the big discovery which never seems to come". Now it was established. Dawson died in 1916 a happy man.

The exact nature of his happiness must remain in doubt. The Piltdown finds were forgeries, Piltdown man a temporarily successful hoax.

As discoveries of other early men and pre-men accumulated, it became increasingly difficult to fit the discoveries in Sussex into the pattern that was emerging. Piltdown man remained an eccentric. It is interesting to read general accounts written in the period 1920–50 and to compare their differing attempts to deal with this situation.

Between 1949 and 1953 the truth was established by the use of newly-developed scientific tests. The skull fragments are perhaps no more than 1,000 years old, the jaw is that of a modern ape—probably an orang-utan, the bone implement had been carved within the last 100 years. Associated remains, animal bones and so on, had come from Tunisia, Malta and Suffolk. Nothing had come from the Piltdown site. The materials had been treated, the teeth artificially ground down to the required extent, most of the bones stained with bichromate of potash.

One mystery had been solved, another had been set up. Who had perpetrated what the modern investigators described in a scientific paper as "a most elaborate and carefully prepared hoax" —and why?

It is generally agreed that Woodward was innocent and that the whole affair was the work either of Dawson or of some unknown third party who was himself hoaxing Dawson. This second possibility is argued in *The Piltdown Fantasy*, by F. Vere. This is not possible to disprove, but there is no evidence for the existence of such a person, possessing the necessary skills and freedom of access to the site.

On the other hand, there is evidence which points to Dawson. He was interested in 'intermediate forms' of many types and had indeed discovered a genuine one within his own specialized field of paleaontology. He had the requisite knowledge and skills, he had access to the Piltdown site and to sources from which he could obtain his 'evidence'. In 1913 another amateur archaeologist had accidentally come across flints and bottles of brown stain on Dawson's desk. Most fascinating of all, there have come to light some notes written by a bank clerk and part-time archaeologist, Morris. One comment reads "Stained by C. Dawson with intent to defraud (all)—H.M." Another records "Judging from an overheard conversation, there is every reason to suppose that the 'canine tooth' found at P. Down was imported from France. Watch C. Dawson. Kind regards."

And the motive? It would be a satisfying answer to see the affair as a black comedy with the respectable solicitor deliberately planting the time bomb that would destroy the reputation of the professionals and smiling at the private joke as he died. It seems more likely, though, that the motive was ambition, the desire to gain the reputation of having made "the big discovery which" as he had told Woodward in 1909 "never seems to come".

Dawson may not, in his own eyes, have been dishonest. He manufactured what he believed to be the truth. A real Piltdown man, he was convinced, would one day be discovered, with the characteristics of his private prototype. Why should he not earn the reputation of discovering what he knew to be true?

If this were his motive, there is a further ironical turn of the screw. Dawson's theories were wrong. Early man and pre-man seems in general to have possessed an ape-like skull and a more human jaw, and not *vice-versa* as he believed.

The destruction of Piltdown man in the fifties symbolizes dramatically the opening of the latest phase in archaeological discovery, a phase in which there rules supreme the scientific detective and the expert witness.

Some of the techniques applied to archaeological investigation during the twentieth cenetury have been indicated in earlier chapters. The range is remarkable, extending from physics to biology, from aeroplanes to submarines, from cameras to computers.

First in order of time was the use of aerial photography, a by-product of the First World War. As early as 1891 there had been a scheme, wrecked on the shoals of officialdom, to photograph the ruined cities of Agra in India from balloons, while in 1906 photographs of Stonehenge were actually taken from a military balloon. During the war the Germans photographed remains in the Sinai desert, while an English colonel was doing the same thing in Mesopotamia. "Unfortunately," the latter wrote, with what one feels to be characteristic phlegm, "I was shot down and captured before being able to make a detailed survey. . . ."

So far, photographs had been taken of ruins perfectly visible on the ground. These photographs provided literally a bird's eye view, instantly comprehensible, of the complex relationships between the different parts of a site. The next development in aerial photography furnished a very different and even more valuable type of information.

It had long been realized that shadows and crop-markings indicated the presence of remains not normally visible—see, for instance, the remarks of William Stukeley already quoted in this chapter. The driving force behind the widespread use of air photographs was O. G. S. Crawford (1886–1957), a former military air photographer who became Archaeology Officer of the Ordnance Survey. He has written: "The birth of the new study in England may be said to date from 1922 when Air-Commodore Clark Hall observed certain curious marks on R.A.F. air-photographs taken in Hampshire. With him must be mentioned Flight-Lieutenant Haslam, who took a number of photographs near Winchester showing what turned out to be Celtic fields."[1] The new tool proved invaluable. Reference has been made in Chapter IV to the first dramatic discovery, that of the hitherto unsuspected existence of Woodhenge, made in 1925.

In 1946 Professor Willard Libby discovered the existence of the radio-active isotope of carbon, carbon 14, and realized that the fact that it decayed at a fixed rate implied that all organic remains had built into them a clock that had been set going, as it were, at the moment of death (see Chapter I). The technique was described by him in 1949.

[1] O. G. S. Crawford and A. Keiller, Wessex from the Air (O.U.P., 1928).

About 1958 another device from the laboratories found its way into the archaeologist's tool-chest. The proton magnetometer is a sensitive indicator of variations in the magnetism of the earth's surface. These variations can be caused by the presence of iron objects lying hidden below the surface. More significant for the archaeologist is the fact that the particles of iron oxide in baked clay also produce a magetic field which can be detected by the magnetometer. Kilns, pottery, household hearths, the footings of buildings that have been burnt down—all can be detected.

Consequently in 1959 M. J. Aitken was able to begin a talk on what was then Network Three of the B.B.C. with the surprising words: "Last spring, in the fields bordering the site of the Roman town of Durobrivae, near Peterborough in Northamptonshire, I measured the speed of gyration of the nucleus of the hydrogen atom; that is, a proton. I measured this speed at five-foot intervals over a large area, and in one spot I found that it was a little faster than elsewhere. A test-hole was dug and at a yard down we found the upper rim of a Romano-British pottery kiln." Later that year, working at the Iron Age hill-fort of Bredon Hill near Tewkesbury, the speaker was able to pin-point ninety pits in five days, although nothing was visible on the surface of the ground.

The botanist and the biologist are also contributing to archaeological knowledge. Reference has already been made in Chapter I to the very important part played by pollen analysis in the reconstruction of the changing pattern of vegetation.

In the sixties a Medical Research Council Team under Dr. A. E. Mourant working on the files of the Blood Donor Service, found that in the lowland zone of Britain 40 per cent of samples were of blood group A. In the highland zone of Scotland, Ireland and North Wales, however, over 50 per cent were of blood group O. It seems reasonable to correlate that lowland group with late invaders, such as the Anglo-Saxons, and the highland group with the survival there of Celtic or pre-Celtic groups. Similar work in other countries has already made it possible to produce a map of Europe, showing tentatively the distribution of blood groups, which seems to fit in well with the prehistory of the area.

Medical analysis of prehistoric remains has revealed the fact—cheering or disheartening, according to the light in which one views it—that from the earliest times man has been subject to most of the diseases from which he suffers today, in so far as these can be determined from the surviving remains. Analysis of bones with reference to the probable age at death reveals what one writer has termed "a bleak view of ancient societies".[1] It would appear that, as least down to the close of Mesolithic times, over 80 per cent of any community had died at or before the age of 30. The brightest feature of the medical reports is that dental disease was low—6 per cent in Neolithic times, falling to 2 or 3 per cent in the Bronze Age and then rising through the Iron Age to a peak of 10 per cent under the Romans.

In central Italy the Etruscans constructed rock-cut tombs beneath the surface of the earth. In some places these lie thick on the ground. It is difficult to decide which would be worth excavating. Carlo Lerici of Milan has developed an instrument that can provide the answer. A hole is drilled into the ground at the centre of a possible site, thus piercing the rock roof of the tomb. A tube is inserted and then a rod with a camera at the end is lowered through the tube. The camera can be rotated, photographs taken by flash, and then the camera withdrawn. A study of the photographs taken with the help of this ingenious periscope enables a decision to be made as to whether to carry out an excavation or to examine another site, perhaps more rewarding.

The archaeologist now peers not only into the earth of Italy, but also into the Mediterranean sea. Underwater archaeology has been developed since the Second World War by the free diver using aqua-lung or similar equipment and clearing his sites by the use of the air-lift, a machine like an underwater vacuum-cleaner.

Within the Mediterranean area discoveries have been numerous and widespread. Before the new techniques were used, old-fashioned divers had made only two archaeological finds: by 1958 a French archaeologist was able to announce that twenty wrecks had been inspected off the coast of Provence alone.

The Mediterranean finds are not prehistoric. They date from the period when England was still in the Bronze or Iron Age, but when southern Europe was already at a more advanced stage of civilization. The earliest important wreck dates from about 1200 B.C. This was that of a ship carrying copper from the mines in Cyprus, which sank off Cape Gelidonya in southern Turkey. It was fully investigated in 1960 by George Bass, leading a team from the University of Pennsylvania. In the western Mediterranean much of the pioneer work has been carried out by the well-known undersea explorer Jacques-Yves Cousteau.

Within the strict limits of prehistory, work has been in progress at Lake Neuchâtel in connection with the lake dwellings

[1] C. Wells, *Bones, Bodies and Disease* (Thames and Hudson, 1964).

there and in the British Isles attempts have been made to identify the foundations of lake dwellings in Loch Lomond.

The twentieth century has been marked not only by the application to archaeological research of scientific methods derived from other disciplines, but also by the carrying-out of increasingly complex campaigns of investigation. Recently there has been a tendency for some at least of these campaigns to be supported financially by outside bodies, itself a sign of the growing popularity of archaeology among the general public.

Thus when, in the late sixties, it was decided to conduct an intensive excavation at South Cadbury, grants were received from, among others, the Pilgrim Trust, the University of Wales, the Society of Antiquaries, the Honourable Society of the Knights of the Round Table, the Cadbury Brothers Charitable Fund, the Morland Charitable Trust, and *The Observer* newspaper—a list representing very varied interests. At Silbury Hill the investigations in 1968–9 were organized and financed by B.B.C.2. In 1970 plans were announced for the establishment of a farm to be worked by Iron Age techniques. The suggested site is at Butser Hill to the west of road A3 south of Petersfield. Those involved in the scheme include both Southampton University and Hampshire County Council. In February 1970 *The Guardian* reported: "There are 57 acres to Butser Hill and right now they look attractive and half wild. If everything goes well oxen will be ploughing that dry valley, yoked as they were 2,300 years ago, hauling bow ards and crook ards, which were the forefathers of our plough. There will be thatched houses built precisely to prehistoric plan, and a granary on stilts. There will be saddle-querns for grinding corn and weighted frame looms for weaving wool. There will be a hedged enclosure and its vegetation will be only what the early Britons knew." If this scheme comes to fruition—and there is no reason why it should not be practicable, the Danes already have something similar in operation—yet another new approach to our prehistory will have been made.

Besides the application of new techniques and the initiation of more elaborate projects there has naturally also been a continual ferment of theoretical deduction from the hard facts obtained. Most of this is not relevant to the ordinary traveller's interests, but two developments of the last seventy years have profoundly affected the archaeologists' approach to British prehistory and are reflected in the display cases of any modern museum.

The first is the recognition that virtually every prehistoric phase in Britain owed its origin, directly or indirectly, to the arrival of immigrants from the mainland of Europe who introduced processes and products already well-established in the lands from which they came.

This concept, vital to a rational prehistory of Britain, was first outlined in a paper read to the British Association in Belfast by the Honourable John Abercomby. He spoke with special reference to the Beaker people, but his thesis clearly had general application and it will be clear from the present book how universal has been the part played by the forces of trade and migration in British prehistory.

The implications were developed by Sir Cyril Fox in his essay on *The Personality of Britain*, first published in 1932. If invaders and traders were the prime source of Britain's prehistoric development, then it was important to consider what aspects these islands presented to the new men. They set sail from three European coastal areas: the North Sea zone, the Channel zone, and the Atlantic zone of Western France, Spain and Portugal. If they landed in southern or eastern Britain they encountered the relatively 'easy' lowland area. If they made their landfall in the north or west they entered the highland area. Each played its part over the centuries. The concept of these two differing zones is examined in slightly more detail in Chapter II.

The second major shift in emphasis has been the progressively rapid breakdown of the 'three-age system'—Stone, Bronze, Iron. Until the mid-twenties the tendency was to subdivide these three ages into progressively smaller compartments—the Bronze Age into four or five successive cultures, the European Iron Age into five, and so on. Up to a point this worked well, and it remains the basic framework for any general discussion. Guide-books and other information issued by the Ministry of Works continue to use this terminology, and the ordinary traveller will still find it the most useful foundation on which to build.

Professionals, however, have over the last forty years become increasingly dissatisfied. Technological terms were being used to define chronological periods. Even within the elementary limits of this book it has become clear that one cannot speak of 'Bronze Age Britain' when people in different parts of these islands were at the same moment in time at differing stages of development—Mesolithic, Secondary Neolithic and Early Bronze 'periods' coexisting, so that one has to specify whether one is speaking of the far north of Scotland, of Yorkshire or of Wessex.

The modern archaeologist prefers to approach his objects rather in the manner in which a botanist approaches plants, and he has indeed begun to take over the word 'taxonomy' from natural history to indicate classification according to type, with no reference to culture or date. Passing progressively from the known to the unknown, the archaeologist describes an object in terms of the place where it was found, its type, its date, its relationship to other objects within this description, and finally gives an over-all historical interpretation. It is a far cry from the nineteenth-century enthusiasts, from the country parson and the casual squire, from the years around 1850 when a local poet could celebrate the activities of Thomas Bateman of Youlgreave in Derbyshire with the lines

> Uprise ye then, our barrow-digging men,
> For 'tis our opening day.

As archaeological methods of investigation and interpretation improve one might at first thought expect the number of perfectly preserved archaeological sites to increase. Second thoughts provide several reasons why this happy state of affairs is not achieved. The fact is sometimes overlooked that an archaeological investigation, by its very nature, can never leave a site as it has found it. The entire structure may have been removed. The wrong questions may have been asked, the right ones never posed. Archaeologists are themselves well aware of this—see the extracts from General Pitt-Rivers given above—but the dilemma remains. A sort of solution is to excavate only part of a site and to leave the rest to the tender mercies of later generations.

A different danger comes from the increasing pace and scope of man's interference with the landscape. Vandalism in the name of fashion or efficiency is nothing new. In the nineteenth century on the top of the passage grave at Dowth, not far from New Grange in Eire, "a modern structure, a *tea-house* was erected by the late eccentric Lord Netterville" recorded Sir William Wilde, the father of Oscar Wilde, in his book *The Beauties of the Boyne*. The comments of Stukeley on the treatment of remains in the Avebury area and at Dorchester have been given in Chapters IV and V.

The removal of standing stones and similar obstacles is by no means confined to Britain. On the island of Rügen in the Baltic there were 229 megalithic tombs recorded in 1827, while by the 1930s there were only forty still left.

Today remains are better guarded against destruction by individuals, but they have little chance if they stand in the way of
'development'.

Far-reaching plans and modern machinery combine to move
great piles of earth from one place to another. In the course of
these activities unexpected archaeological finds are not uncommon,
but there is rarely time for a complete investigation before the
sites disappear, probably for ever. Typical is this item from the
first months of 1970: "Archaeologists investigating an Iron Age
settlement which was discovered during motorway work at Chris-
ton, near Weston-super-Mare in Somerset, are removing 14 skeletons this weekend before bulldozers reach the site." Something,
clearly, has been discovered that might not have come to light at
this time, equally clearly something is in process of being lost.

The bureaucrat nods to the intellectual, but he respects the
technologist and if the latter were to suggest that a motorway, a
line of pylons, or a nuclear power station were best sited alongside, for instance, Stonehenge—why, beside Stonehenge the 'im-
provements' would be placed.

There is quite a different sort of danger that arises from the
tendency to tidy up too much. The Ministry of Public Building
and Works is an invaluable watchdog and custodian, yet it has
been argued by some archaeologists that Hadrian's Wall has
suffered at that department's hands more than ever it did from
the forces of barbarism and the weather.

Part of the trouble is that mere numbers of visitors can destroy
the whole setting of a site unless they move with tact and delicacy.
"Every age", Jacquetta Hawkes has observed, "has the Stonehenge
it deserves—or desires." We have one that is rapidly becoming
an island surrounded by concrete posts, gravel paths, ashphalt car-
parks, public lavatories and bookstalls. They are a by-product of
the pressure of public curiosity.

FURTHER INFORMATION

Maps are essential. Almost all sites can be identified on the one-inch sheets of the Ordnance Survey. In addition the Survey produces some specialized maps:

1. "Ancient Britain. A map of the major visible antiquities of Great Britain older than A.D. 1066." is on a scale of about 10 miles to one inch. The South Sheet covers England as far north as Scarborough. The remainder of England, and the whole of Scotland, is on the companion North Sheet.
2. "Neolithic Wessex."
3. "Southern Britain in the Iron Age."

The museums mentioned in the text will be found in the index under the catchword museums.

The guides produced by the Ministry of Public Buildings and Works are invaluable for individual sites. The Ministry also produces a series of Regional Guides to Ancient Monuments. Ministry publications are published by Her Majesty's Stationery Office, which is also responsible for a series of Guides to the National Parks, which contain surveys of the prehistory of the areas with which they deal.

The least technical of archaeological journals is a newcomer: *Current Archaeology* (six issues per annum, present subscription £1 (published from 128 Barnsbury Road, London, N.1.

The Council for British Archaeology publishes during the summer months a *Calendar of Excavations*, giving details of work in progress and of sites at which help is welcomed. It can be obtained, quite cheaply, from the Council of British Archaeology, 8 St. Andrew's Place, London N.W.1.

Books include the following general surveys which adopt four different methods of approach:

J. G. D. Clark, *Prehistoric England* (Batsford, 1963)

J. Hawkes, *A Guide to the Prehistoric and Roman Monuments of England and Wales* (Chatto, 1961)

D. Roe, *Prehistory* (Macmillan, 1969)

N. Thomas, *A Guide to Prehistoric England* (Batsford, 1960)

Two valuable groups of books are the relevant volumes in the Thames and Hudson Ancient Peoples and Places series, and the Regional Archaeologies series published by Heinemann.

For Ireland, Scotland and Wales possible introductions are:

E. E. Evans, *Prehistoric and Early Christian Ireland* (Batsford, 1966)

R. W. Feachem, *Prehistoric Scotland* (Batsford, 1963)

I. Ll. Foster and L. Alcock, *Prehistoric and Early Wales* (Routledge and Kegan Paul, 1965)

On the development of archaeology, see:

G. Daniel, *The Origins and Growth of Archaeology* (Penguin, 1967)

T. D. Kendrick, *British Antiquity* (Methuen, 1950)

The following books deal mainly with individual aspects or areas:

P. Ashbee, *The Bronze Age Round Barrow in Britain* (Phoenix, 1960)

R. J. C. Atkinson, *Stonehenge* (Penguin, 1960)

R. J. C. Atkinson, *Stonehenge and Avebury and Neighbouring Monuments* (H.M.S.O., 1968)

R. R. Clarke, *East Anglia* (Thames and Hudson, 1960)

O. G. S. Crawford and A. Keiller, *Wessex from the Air* (O.U.P., 1928)

P. Fowler, *Wessex* (Heinemann, 1967)

Sir Cyril Fox *The Personality of Britain* (National Museum of Wales, 1952)

Lady Aileen Fox *South-west England* (Thames and Hudson, 1964)

G. Daniel, *The Megalithic Builders of Western Europe* (Hutchinson, 1958)

J. du Plat Taylor, *Marine Archaeology* (Hutchinson, 1965)

L. V. Grinsell, *The Archaeology of Wessex* (Methuen, 1958)

I. Longworth, *Yorkshire* (Heinemann, 1967)

Dartmoor (National Park Guides Number One H.M.S.O., 1957)

K. S. Painter, *The Severn Basin* (Heinemann, 1967)

S. Piggott, *Ancient Europe* (Edinburgh U.P., 1965)

S. Piggott, *The Druids* (Thames and Hudson, 1968)

S. Piggott, *The Neolithic Cultures of the British Isles* (C.U.P., 1954)

T. G. E. Powell, *The Celts* (Thames and Hudson, 1958)

J. F. S. Stone, *Wessex Before the Celts* (Thames and Hudson, 1958)

C. Wells, *Bones, Bodies and Disease* (Thames and Hudson, 1964)

R. E. M. Wheeler, *Maiden Castle, Dorset* (O.U.P., 1943)

INDEX OF SITES

GENERAL INDEX